Action For A Change

ALSO AVAILABLE:

To the students
who created the first PIRGs,
and to students nationwide,
who will create many more,
we dedicate this book.

A STUDENT'S MANUAL FOR PUBLIC INTEREST ORGANIZING

by RALPH NADER and DONALD ROSS
with Joseph Highland

GROSSMAN PUBLISHERS NEW YORK 1972

Action For A Change

Revised Edition

ACKNOWLEDGMENT

There are many other people who worked hard to make this book possible, and we are indebted to them. Foremost among them are James D. Welch and Caren Calish, whose nationwide travels helped bring the idea of Public Interest Research Groups to many campuses.

Special thanks also are due to Brent English (a co-author of the first edition), Kate Blackwell, and Ruth Fort for editorial assistance, and to Connie Jo Smith, Karen Klinginsmith, and Susan Perry for assistance in producing the manuscript.

CONTENTS

Part One

TOWARD AN
INITIATORY DEMOCRACY

This country has more problems than it should tolerate and more solutions than it uses. Few societies in the course of human history have faced such a situation: most are in the fires without the water to squelch them. Our society has the resources and the skills to keep injustice at bay and to elevate the human condition to a state of enduring compassion and creative fulfillment. How we go about using the resources and skills has consequences which extend well beyond our national borders to all the earth's people.

How do we go about this? The question has been asked and answered in many ways throughout the centuries. Somehow, the answers, even the more lasting ones, whether conforming or defiant, affect the reality of living far less than the intensity of their acceptance would seem to indicate. Take the conventional democratic creeds, for example. Many nations have adopted them, and their principles have wide popular reception. But the theories are widely separated from practice. Power and wealth remain concentrated, decisions continue to be made by the few, victims have little representation in thousands of forums which affect their rights, livelihoods, and futures. And societies like ours, which have produced much that is good, are developing new perils, stresses, and deprivations of unprecedented scope and increasing

3

risk. As the technologies of war and economics become more powerful and pervasive, the future, to many people, becomes more uncertain and fraught with fear. Past achievements are discounted or depreciated as the quality of life drifts downward in numerous ways. General economic growth produces costs which register, like the silent violence of poverty and pollution, with quiet desperation, ignored by entrenched powers, except in their rhetoric.

But the large institutions' contrived nonaccountability, complex technologies, and blameworthy indifference have not gone unchallenged, especially by the young. The very magnitude of our problems has reminded them of old verities and taught them new values. The generation gap between parents and children is in part a difference in awareness and expectation levels. Parents remember the Depression and are thankful for jobs. The beneficiaries—their children—look for more meaningful work and wonder about those who still do not have jobs in an economy of plenty because of rebuffs beyond their control. Parents remember World War II and what the enemy could have done to America; children look on the Vietnam War and other similar wars and wonder what America has done to other people and what, consequently, she is doing to herself. To parents, the noxious plume from factory smokestacks was the smell of the payroll; children view such sights as symbols of our domestic chemical warfare that is contaminating the air, water, and soil now and for many years hence. Parents have a more narrow concept of neighborhood; children view Earth as a shaky ship requiring us all to be our brother's keeper, regardless of political boundaries.

In a sense, these themes, or many like them, have distinguished the split between fathers and sons for generations; very often the resolution is that the sons become like the fathers. The important point is not that such differences involve a statistically small number of the young—historic changes, including the American Revolution, have always come through minorities—but that conditions are indeed serious, and a new definition of work is needed to deal with them.

That new kind of work is a new kind of citizenship. The word "citizenship" has a dull connotation—which is not surprising, given its treatment by civics books and the way it has been neglected. But the role of the citizen is obviously central to democracy, and it is time to face up to the burdens and liberations of citizenship.

Democratic systems are based on the principle that all power comes from the people. The administration of governmental power begins to erode this principle in practice immediately. The inequality of wealth, talent, ambition, and fortune in the society works its way into the governmental process which is supposed to be distributing evenhanded justice, resources, and opportunities. Can the governmental process resist such pressures as the chief trustee of structured democratic power given it by the consent of the governed? Only to the degree to which the governed develop ways to apply their generic power in meticulous and practical ways on a continual basis. A citizenship of wholesale delegation and abdication to public and private power systems, such as prevails now, makes such periodic checks as elections little more than rituals. It permits tweedledum and tweedledee choices that put mostly indistinguishable candidates above meaningful issues and programs. It facilitates the overwhelming dominance of the pursuit of private or special interests, to the detriment of actions bringing the greatest good to the greatest number. It breeds despair, discouragement, resignation, cynicism, and all that is involved in the "You can't fight City Hall" syndrome. It constructs a society which has thousands of full-time manicurists and pastrymakers but less than a dozen citizen-specialists fighting full time against corporate water contamination or to get the government to provide food (from bulging warehouses) for millions of undernourished Americans.

Building a new way of life around citizenship action must be the program of the immediate future. The ethos that looks upon citizenship as an avocation or opportunity must be replaced with the commitment to citizenship as an obligation, a continual receiver of our time, energy, and skill. And that commitment must be transformed into a strategy of action that develops instruments of change while it focuses on what needs to be done. This is a critical point. Too often, people who are properly outraged over injustice concentrate so much on decrying the abuses and demanding the desired reforms that they never build the instruments to accomplish their objectives in a lasting manner.

There are three distinct roles through which effective citizenship activity can be channeled. First is the full-time professional citizen, who makes his career by applying his skills to a wide range of public problems. These citizens are not part of any governmental, corporate, or union institutions. Rather they are independently based, working *on* institutions to improve and reshape them or replace them with improved ways of achieving just missions. With their full-time base, they are able to mobilize and encourage part-time citizen activity.

With shorter workweeks heading toward the four-day week, part-time involvement can become an integral part of the good life for blue- and white-collar workers. Certainly many Americans desire to find the answers to two very recurrent questions: "What can I do to improve my community?" and "How do I go about doing it?" The development of the mechanics of taking a serious abuse, laying it bare before the public, proposing solutions, and generating the necessary coalitions to see these solutions through —these steps metabolize the latent will of people to contribute to their community and count as individuals rather than as cogs in large organizational wheels.

The emergence of capabilities and outlets for citizenship expression has profound application to the third form of citizenship

TOWARD AN INITIATORY DEMOCRACY

activity—on-the-job citizenship. Consider the immense knowledge of waste, fraud, negligence, and other misdeeds which employees of corporations, governmental agencies, and other bureaucracies possess. Most of this country's abuses are secrets known to thousands of insiders, at times right down to the lowest paid worker. A list of Congressional exposures in the poverty, defense, consumer fraud, environmental, job safety, and regulatory areas over the past five years would substantiate that observation again and again. The complicity of silence, of getting along by going along, of just taking orders, of "mum's the word" has been a prime target of student activism and a prime factor leading students to exercise their moral concern. When large organizations dictate to their employees, and when their employees, in turn, put ethical standards aside and perform their work like minions—that is a classic prescription for institutional irresponsibility. The individual must have an opportunity and a right to blow the whistle on his organization—to make higher appeals to outside authorities, to professional societies, to citizen groups—rather than be forced to condone illegality, consumer hazards, oppression of the disadvantaged, seizure of public resources, and the like. The ethical whistle-blower may be guided by the Golden Rule, a refusal to aid and abet crimes, occupational standards of ethics, or a genuine sense of patriotism. To deny him or her the protections of the law and supportive groups is to permit the institutionalization of organizational tyranny throughout the society at the grass roots where it matters.

On-the-job citizenship, then, is a critical source of information, ideas, and suggestions for change. Everybody who has a job knows of some abuses which pertain to that industry, commerce, or agency. Many would like to do something about these abuses, and their numbers will grow to the extent that they believe their assistance will improve conditions and not just expose them to being called troublemakers or threaten them with losing their

7

jobs. They must believe that if they are right there will be someone to defend them and protect their right to speak out. A GM Fisher Body inspector went public on defectively welded Chevrolets that allowed exhaust gases, including carbon monoxide, to seep into passenger compartments. He had previously reported the defects repeatedly to plant managers without avail. In 1969 GM recalled over two million such Chevrolets for correction. The inspector still works at the plant, because union and outside supporters made it difficult for GM to reward such job citizenship with dismissal.

The conventional theory—that change by an institution in the public interest requires external pressure—should not displace the potential for change when that pressure forges an alliance with people of conscience *within* the institution. When the managerial elite knows that it cannot command its employees' complete allegiance to its unsavory practices, it will be far less likely to engage in such actions. This is a built-in check against the manager's disloyalty to the institution. Here is seen the significant nexus between full-time and part-time citizens with on-the-job citizens. It is a remarkable reflection on the underdevelopment of citizenship strategies that virtually no effort has been directed toward ending these divisions with a unison of action. But then, every occupation has been given expertise and full-time practitioners except the most important occupation of all—citizenship. Until unstructured citizen power is given the tools for impact, structured power, no matter how democratic in form, will tend toward abuse, indifference, or sloth. Such deterioration has occurred not only in supposedly democratic governments but in unions, cooperatives, motor clubs, and other membership groups. For organizations such as corporations, which are admittedly undemocratic (even toward their shareholders), the necessity for a professional citizenship is even more compelling.

How, then, can full-time, part-time, and on-the-job citizens work together on a wide, permanent, and effective scale? A number of models around the country, where young lawyers and other specialists have formed public interest firms to promote or defend citizen-consumer rights vis-à-vis government and corporate behavior, show the way. Given their tiny numbers and resources, their early impact has been tremendous. There are now a few dozen such people, but there need to be thousands, from all walks and experiences in life. What is demanded is a major redeployment of skilled manpower to make the commanding institutions in our society respond to needs which they have repudiated or neglected. This is a life's work for many Americans, and there is no reason why students cannot begin understanding precisely what is involved and how to bring it about.

It may be asked why the burden of such pioneering has to be borne by the young. The short answer is to say that this is the way it has always been. But there is a more functional reason: no other group is possessed of such flexibility, freedom, imagination, and willingness to experiment. Moreover, many students truly desire to be of service to humanity in practical, effective ways. The focused idealism of thousands of students in recent years brings a stronger realism to the instruments of student action outlined in this book. Indeed, this action program could not have been written in the fifties or early sixties. The world—especially the student world—has changed since those years.

Basic to the change is that victims of injustice are rising to a level of recurrent visibility. They are saying in many ways that a just system would allow, if not encourage, victims to attain the power of alleviating their present suffering or future concerns. No longer is it possible to ignore completely the "Other America" of poverty, hunger, discrimination, and abject slums. Nor can the economic exploitation of the consumer be camouflaged by pompous references to the accumulation of goods and services in the American household. For the lines of responsibility between un-

safe automobiles, shoddy merchandise, adulterated or denutri-
tionized foods, and rigged prices with corporate behavior and governmental abdication have become far too clear. Similarly,
environmental breakdowns have reached critical masses of destruction, despoliation, ugliness, and, above all, mounting health
hazards through contaminated water, soil, and air. Growing protests by the most aggrieved have made more situations visible and
have increased student perception of what was observed. Observation has led to participation which in turn has led to engagement.
This sequence has most expressly been true for minorities and
women. The aridity and seeming irrelevance of student course
work has provided a backdrop for even more forceful rebounds
into analyzing the way things are. Parallel with civil rights, antiwar efforts, ecology, and other campus causes, which have ebbed
and flowed, the role of students within universities has become a
stressful controversy which has matured many students and some
faculty in a serious assessment of their relation to these institutions
and to society at large.

This assessment illuminates two conditions. First, it takes too
long to grow up in our culture. Extended adolescence, however it
services commercial and political interests, deprives young people
of their own fulfillment as citizens and of the chance to make valuable contributions to society. Second, contrary to the old edict
that students should stay within their ivory tower before they go
into the cold, cold world, there is every congruence between the
roles of student and citizen. The old distinction will become even
more artificial with the exercise and imaginative use of the eigh-
teen- to twenty-year-old vote throughout the country.

For the first time, students will have decisive voting power in
many local governments. One does not have to be a political science major to appreciate the depth of resourceful experience and
responsibility afforded by such a role. The quality of electoral politics could be vastly improved, with direct impact on economic

power blocs, if students use the vote intelligently and creatively around the country.

Such a happening is not a foregone conclusion, as those who fought successfully in the past for enfranchisement of other groups learned to their disappointment; but there are important reasons why this enfranchisement of the eighteen- to twenty-year-old could be different. Over a third of the eleven and a half million people in this group are college students with a sense of identity and a geographical concentration for canvassing and voting leverage. Certainly, problems of communication are minimized, and a resurgent educational curriculum can be an intellectually demanding forum for treating the facts and programs which grow into issue-oriented politics in the students' voting capacities.

Full use of voting rights will induce a higher regard for students by older citizens, and elected and appointed officials. It is unlikely that legislators will rise on the floor of the legislature and utter the verbose ridicules wrapped in a smug authoritarian condescension that students are accustomed to hearing. From now on, legislators will pay serious attention to students. Therefore the student vote and the student citizen are intimately connected. Student Public Interest Research Groups (PIRGs) composed of full-time professional advocates and able organizers recruited by and representing students as citizens can have an enormous, constructive impact on society. It could be a new ball game, if the student players avoid the temptations of despair, dropping out, and cynicism.

There are other obstacles which students put in their own way that deserve candid appraisal by all those involved in establishing and directing student PIRGs. These are the shoals of personal piques, ego problems, envy, megalomania, resentment, deception, and other frailties which are distributed among students as they are among other people. On such shoals the best plan and the highest enthusiasm can run aground, or be worn to exhaustion

11

by the attrition of pettiness. Even after the PIRGs are established, these frictions can continue to frustrate and weaken their missions. They will surface at every step—from recruitment to choice of subject matters to the relations with the PIRG professionals. They must be averted at every step with candor, firmness, anticipatory procedures, and a goal-oriented adhesion that reduces such interferences to nuisances. Such nuisances will serve to remind all how important are character, stamina, self-discipline, and consistency of behavior with the values espoused to the success of the PIRG idea and its repercussive impact.

Self-discipline must be emphasized in this student age of free-think and free-do. Many kinds of cop-outs come in the garb of various liberated styles which sweep over campuses. Clearly, there has to be, for the purposes discussed in this volume, a reversal of the dictum "If you desire to do it, you should do it" to "If you should do it, you should desire to do it." Such an attitude makes for persistence and incisiveness. It forces the asking of the important questions and the pursuit of the pertinent inquiries. It develops an inner reserve that refuses to give up and that thinks of ways for causes to be continually strengthened for sustained breakthroughs. The drive for a firmly rooted *initiatory* democracy is basic to all democratic participations and institutions, but initiatory democracy does not rest on the firmaments of wealth or bureaucratic power. It rests on conviction, work, intellect, values, and a willingness to sacrifice normal indulgences for the opportunity to come to grips as never before with the requisites of a just society. It also rests on a communion with the people for whom this effort is directed.

More and more students today are realistic about power, and they reject merely nominal democratic forms which shield or legitimize abuses. The great debates of the past over where power should be placed—in private or public hands—appear sterile to them. Students are suspicious of power wherever it resides because they know how such power can corrode and corrupt regardless of what crucible—corporate, governmental, or union—contains it. Moreover, the systematic use of public power by private interests against the citizenry, including the crude manipulation of the law as an instrument of oppression, has soured many of the brightest students against the efficacy of both government and law. At the same time, however, most concerned students are averse to rigid ideological views which freeze intellects and narrow the choices of action away from adaptability and resiliency.

Such skepticism can become overextended in a form of self-paralysis. I have seen too many students downplay what other students have already accomplished in the past decade with little organization, less funds, and no support. Who began the sit-in movement in civil rights, a little over a decade ago, which led to rapid developments in the law? Four black engineering students. Who dramatized for the nation the facts and issues regarding the relentless environmental contamination in cities and rural America? Students. Who helped mobilize popular opposition to the continuance of the war in Vietnam and, at least, turned official policy toward withdrawal? Who focused attention on the need for change in university policies and obtained many of these changes? Who is enlarging the investigative tradition of the old muckrakers in the Progressive-Populist days at the turn of the century other than student teams of inquiry? Who is calling for and shaping a more relevant and empirical education that understands problems, considers solutions, and connects with people? Who poured on the pressure to get the eighteen- to twenty-year-old vote? A tiny minority of students.

Still the vast majority of their colleagues are languishing in colossal wastes of time, developing only a fraction of their potential, and woefully underpreparing themselves for the world they are entering in earnest. Student PIRGs can inspire with a large array of projects which demand the development of analytic and value training for and by students. These projects will show that knowledge and its uses are seamless webs which draw from all disciplines at a university and enrich each in a way that arranged interdisciplinary work can never do. The artificial isolations and ennui which embrace so many students will likely dissolve before the opportunity to relate education to life's quests, problems, and realities. The one imperative is for students to avoid a psychology of prejudgment in this period of their lives when most are as free to choose and act as they will ever be, given the constraints of careers and family responsibilities after graduation. The most astonishing aspect of what has to be done in this country by citizens is that it has never been tried. What students must do, in effect, is create their own careers in these undertakings.

The problems of the present and the risks of the future are deep and plain. But let it not be said that this generation refused to give up so little in order to achieve so much.

—R.N.

Part Two

1 STUDENT ACTIVISM: THE PAST—THE POTENTIAL

The student movement has come a long way from that day in February 1960 when four bible-carrying black students sat down at a lunch counter in Greensboro, South Carolina, and refused to move until served. They and the thousands of black and white civil rights workers who followed their example were abused and in some cases arrested, beaten, or murdered. Yet the protests continued until the most visible racial restrictions were eliminated by the Civil Rights Act of 1964.

In the recent history of the student movement the academic year 1964–65 appears as a watershed. In the fall, the Free Speech Movement erupted at Berkeley; in the spring, the first Vietnam Teach-in at Michigan signaled the start of five years of intense student activism. The basic principle of student rights enunciated at Berkeley echoed across the country as school after school discarded old traditions and turned to the future. At the same time, the Vietnam protest movement swelled and hundreds of thousands of graduates charted their college careers with the landmarks of protest—the Pentagon March in 1967, the Chicago protests in 1968, and the great Washington and San Francisco peace marches in 1968 and 1969. The decade of activism ended tragi-

17

.

cally with the murders at Kent and Jackson State and the collapse of the great student strike of 1970.

In the first years of the 1970's, the meetings, rallies, and protests that stirred the campus during the 1960's were submerged. In their place was a willingness among many students to forget protest, ignore social concerns, and return to the ivory-tower isolation of their classrooms or their personal utopias. The civil rights movement, the antiwar movements, and the struggle for student rights seemed to have left mostly disillusionment, despair, and apathy.

But if the lessons learned in the student movement of the 1960's were bitter, they were nonetheless instructive. They showed that students have enormous resources at their disposal, that they have the potential for providing the direction, the manpower, the energy, and the ideals to make an impact on the rest of society. In the 1960's students led the way onto the freedom buses. They were among the first to recognize the horrors of the Vietnam War. Earth Day and its sequels centered on the nation's campuses. Today, no less than then, students can give direction to the country. Students of the 1970's inherit this potential as well as the disillusionment of their collective past. But they have not yet decided what to do with either.

The Problem of Continuity

The apathy and discouragement apparent among many students today is only partly due to their frustration with the system and its meager response to their most vigorous efforts. They are also frustrated by the facts of student life that mitigate against continuity, make it difficult to organize across numerous campuses, and hinder long-range efforts that can carry through with the expectations raised on initiating a program for reform. All student activities, whether academic, political, athletic, or extra-curricular, suffer from a lack of continuity. Other groups suffer from the same problem, but with students it is especially severe. Their stay on campus is punctuated by summer vacations, midterm holidays, exams, papers, and concern with career plans. Seldom are they able to apply all of their efforts to the solution of a particular problem. Thus, student activism tends to be a sporadic response to a crisis situation, often followed by frustration and depression from lack of success.

Students' inability to follow through on a project is most serious in social welfare areas. If projects dealing with people's lives and well-being are dropped in midstream, the consequences are serious. For example, if a ghetto literacy program is discontinued because of summer vacation, people suffer more than if the second annual dance never occurs. In the early 1960's civil rights workers filled the South during vacation period. Projects were started and expectations rose. But in September when the school bell rang, a mass exodus occurred. Students returned to their classrooms, taking experiences with them, but leaving the problems and their solutions far behind.

The campus peace movement has suffered from the same discontinuities. Its yearly progression can be charted on a graph. Activism rises in the fall after details like housing and registration are taken care of, and peaks in mid-November before winter arrives. During December, January, and February activist blood thickens and slows, and a kind of hibernation occurs. The first warm day in March rekindles fervor, and activism is again the fashion until May and the approach of final exams. Summer vacation occasions another three-month lull, and in the fall the whole cycle begins anew. If this description sounds cynical, try to remember a January peace march or a major August demonstration. They are as rare as Pentagon doves.

Unfortunately, social problems rarely adapt themselves to student schedules. The urban ghetto still suffers when students are on vacation. Price fixing, sex discrimination, and deceptive packaging do not cease during exam periods. Even though Earth Day 1970 raised the level of public concern about the quality of the environment, it did not clean the air, strain sewage from rivers, or alleviate other environmental problems. A continuous, focused effort is required even to dent the surface of these problems.

The same situation prevails in the political world. In May 1970 thousands of students journeyed to Washington to protest the Cambodian invasion. But in August when the McGovern-Hatfield Amendment to end the war came to a vote, the halls of Congress were empty of students. The vote didn't fit into the student activist timetable. May Day 1971 and the flurry of protests against the spring 1972 blockade and bombing followed this same pattern. A few days of sustained activity, a brief flurry of energy followed by a return to normality—inaction, lethargy, and unconcern.

A New Student Activism

Some students are beginning to realize that the old strategies and structures of the student movement must be altered to meet new realities. Though the ideals may remain the same, the problems do not. For example, equal opportunity today no longer involves the small Southern motel or movie theatre. It centers on the corporation—distant, highly anonymous, powerful far beyond a cadre of small-town police or angry citizens. The problems today involve more subtle violations of human rights than those which were fought in the past decade—violations of a worker's right to health and safety on the job, a community's right to a clean environment, and a citizen's right to participate in decisions that affect him.

Problems that absorbed students in the 1960's tended to be visible, localized, and susceptible to solutions by direct citizen action. Abuses today tend to be hidden. Discrimination is no longer advertised by a "whites only" sign at a lunch counter. It is often revealed only by painstaking documentation of corporate hiring practices, by searches of government files, or by sophisticated analyses of college board exams. Solutions are also more complex, requiring knowledge of law, economics, and, in the case of environmental abuse, science and engineering.

Take for example the corporate polluter. Sit-ins and marches will not clean up the rivers and the air that he fouls. He is too powerful and there are too many like him. Yet the student has unique access to the resources that can be effective in confronting the polluter. University and college campuses have the means for detecting the precise nature of the industrial effluent, through chemical or biological research. Through research such as they perform every day in the classroom, students can show the effect of the effluent on an entire watershed, and thus alert the community to real and demonstrable dangers to public health—a far more powerful way to arouse public support for a clean environment than a sit-in. Using the expertise of the campus, students can also demonstrate the technological means available for abating the discharge, and thus meet the polluter's argument that he can do nothing to control his pollution. By drawing on the knowledge of economists, students can counter arguments that an industry will go bankrupt or close down if forced to install pollution controls. Law and political science students can investigate the local, state, or federal regulations that may apply to the case, and publicly challenge the responsible agencies to fulfill their legal duties.

Utilizing a variety of disciplines, students can fashion powerful investigative teams to affect an array of problems facing their society. They can study, for example, the economic incentives for community waste recycling, analyze overpackaging, and investigate methods of solid waste disposal—a much more effective and sophisticated approach to the solid waste problem than the more frequent litter cleanup campaign.

Instead of simply decrying race or sex discrimination in employment, students can use surveys, questionnaires, and job interviews to gather hard evidence of discrimination where it exists. Such evidence can serve as the basis for a formal complaint to the Equal Employment Opportunities Commission and for a suit under Title VII of the Civil Rights Act of 1964.

Evidence of price fixing is available in hundreds of government files to the persevering investigator. In the areas of both employment discrimination and price fixing, courts reward successful complainants payment either of attorney's fees, back wages, or damage awards. This is a tangible result that is entirely within the grasp of students.

In the past, student researchers have compiled an impressive record in many areas. A student investigation followed by a critical report precipitated the transformation of the moribund Federal Trade Commission into a more vigorous consumer-oriented agency. Voting drives spearheaded by seventeen- and eighteen-year-olds produced the 26th Amendment of the United States Constitution. A graduate student at the University of Western Ontario, Norvald Fimreite, was the first to report mercury residues in fish caught in the Great Lakes and thereby unleash a nationwide alert on the problems of this deadly chemical in fish.

These approaches are far removed from the older tactics of the student movement, which centered on mass demonstrations, highly publicized confrontations with authorities, and summer projects such as the Mississippi voter registration drives and freedom marches. The new problems require more expertise, lengthy and often arduous research, and tedious interviews with minor bureaucrats. As yet, this prescription for action has found all too few adherents on the campus. Successful FTC investigations and voting drives are the exception rather than the rule. Few students have been willing to exchange the easy paths of sloganeering or indifference for lonely hours in the library and inglorious confrontations with low-level officials. But it is to be remembered that, at least as far as world society and ecology are concerned, the young —the students—will inherit the earth. In a very real sense, it is up to them to prod and to provoke, to research and to act, to assure that something remains worth inheriting.

The Student Public Interest Research Group

Unless continuity, expertise, and direction are joined together, there is little hope that students can bring about social betterment. Unless the cycles of vacation and classes, of home life and campus living, and of rising and falling activity can be eliminated, student movements are doomed to partial success at best. Stagnation is likely to occur if the same stale tactics continue. If things are to get done, a new approach is desperately needed.

Students now need the help of professionals in their social efforts. Professionals can bring not only their expertise—for example, their credentials to practice law in a court—but also the continuity of full-time work on the problems. A coalition of students and professionals can provide a workable vehicle for students to pursue their ideals and apply their talents. At the same time, professionals—lawyers, economists, scientists, and engineers—can provide the direction and staying power, as well as the specialized knowledge that is required.

This is the theory behind a student Public Interest Research Group (PIRG). There is no reason that students cannot hire a full-time professional staff to act as the backbone of their social consciences. With a minimal contribution from each student on a campus, they will have the resources to set up an ongoing organization that will remain stable as student bodies change. Through elected representatives, students from campuses across a state can join in concerted action on problems that concern them. This plan has already met with great success. The first two student Public Interest Research Groups began work in the fall of 1971. As of September 1972, twelve groups were in operation and ten more were in the process of forming.

The idea of students hiring a full-time professional staff to carry out projects is not new. Universities themselves began when groups of students with common interests hired tutors. Later, tutors and students joined together to hire administrators to provide support. Today free schools are being developed at which students hire teachers to aid them in learning. More recently, student government officers have hired professionals to run student union buildings and to provide athletic and cultural services on campus. In California, Texas, and other states, students have hired lobbyists and lawyers to represent them before the legislature and the courts. The logical extension is that students should hire a full-time staff to help them work on issues affecting consumers, the environment, and other public problems.

Special interest groups like trade associations, professional associations, unions, and education associations already hire professional advocates to represent their vested economic interests. Decision-makers in government too frequently are cut off from all influences save those exerted by these special interest groups. Public interest advocates hired by students would provide a needed voice for unrepresented public interests. They would also open the doors of government to ordinary citizens who usually do not have the time or talent to find their way through complex public agencies.

Student investigators working with professionals can begin to probe deeply into the activities of city and state administrative agencies to ascertain whether they are carrying out their legislative mandates. They can scrutinize the marketplace for evidence of unfair trade practices. They can examine factory conditions to uncover occupational health or safety hazards. They can study taxation systems to determine equitability. They can act as monitors to guard against discrimination on grounds of race, sex, or creed. Finally, they will stand ready to act in new areas affecting the general public as those areas emerge.

2 THE MEANS

The notion of students and professionals combining their energy and expertise to solve social problems may at first seem uncomplicated and straightforward. But questions of how to mobilize this team immediately arise.

The first decision to be made is the size of the student constituency. Should students from only one campus band together? From several? Should the group be regional, statewide, or wider still? A number of considerations indicate that statewide or regional organizations of students and professionals is best.

1. In a medium to large state a PIRG needs a staff of eight to twelve full-time workers if it is to play a major role. Few schools, acting alone, are large enough to support a staff of this size. Moreover, a single campus PIRG is unlikely to command the attention of the press or the support of a statewide student constituency. Also, there is more of a chance to gain support from the general population when people can see large and small, public and private, conservative and liberal schools united under a common program. There are other problems associated with a single campus PIRG. Attracting professionals may be more difficult since

the group ordinarily will have less power and range. For these reasons it is better to construct the PIRG on a multi-campus foundation.

2. The states, unlike municipalities and counties, are *sovereign units of government,* subject only to the federal and state constitutions. Thus the legal and political actions of a PIRG are most suitably directed either to the states or to the federal government itself, since in these governments power resides. Even in those cases where a PIRG would most practicably be organized regionally (see point 4 below), the PIRG should maintain an office in the state capital.

3. It is always possible to combine the activities of two or more PIRGs when the issues involved require it. For example, four state public interest groups combined resources during the summer of 1972 to help form the Educational Testing Service (ETS) Study Project. A study of pollution in Lake Michigan might require the combined efforts of PIRGs in Michigan, Indiana, Illinois, and Wisconsin. But to combine several state PIRGs administratively would serve no useful purpose and it might limit their scope of action and create an unwieldy bureaucracy. Even if schools in Maine, New Hampshire, and Vermont decided to unite to form a single PIRG, the group still would have to establish offices in Augusta, Concord, and Montpelier. So no administrative advantage would be gained.

4. The final reason for a multi-school, one-state PIRG is that, in most cases, students within a state share a community of interest that may not be found in other configurations of the PIRG. Most students in public universities—by far the largest group of students in the nation—are citizens of the state they study in. In some states, however, statewide organization would be impracticably cumbersome. There are, for example, over seven hundred thousand students in the California community colleges alone, plus hundreds of thousands more in state and private col-

leges and universities. Moreover, the size and diversity of California, like Massachusetts, Pennsylvania, and New York, suggests that regional PIRGs would be best: Northern and Southern California, New York City/Long Island and Upstate New York, and so on.

The above reasons explain why statewide or regional organization is preferable when forming a PIRG. However, if geography, student apathy, or administration conservatism prevents formation of a multi-school organization, a single-school PIRG is feasible. Given the desperate need for citizen action in this country, an unstable, relatively small PIRG is still better than no program at all. What's more, if a PIRG functions well in one school it can easily expand its base to include other schools. In the same way, if a PIRG project encompassing several states should prove desirable, a link-up between independent groups could certainly be arranged.

The second decision which student organizers must make concerns the method of funding which will be used to support the PIRG. The PIRG and its source of support are inextricably linked, since there can be no sustained effort without secure funding. The lack of financial stability was one of the chief causes of discontinuity in previous student efforts, and it remains the major obstacle to student-supported PIRGs. Other university activities are equally dependent on the orderly collections of money. Without financial certainty, academic departments would be a shambles, athletic schedules would collapse, and most other university programs would suffer similar fates. A PIRG is no exception to this rule. Therefore, it is imperative to design a funding system that will provide a solid foundation on which to construct a PIRG.

Funding Systems

There are a variety of possible funding systems capable of raising money to support a PIRG. When the first PIRGs were formed during the 1970–71 academic year, the question of which fund-raising system to use was not of great moment. During the 1971–72 academic year, it became a matter of intense concern on many campuses. Therefore, it is important to consider each system in detail.

VOLUNTARY DONATIONS

Suppose professors were required to obtain their salaries by asking students to make *anonymous*, totally voluntary donations. Or if the school's bond payments had to be redeemed by the proceeds of a few concerts and an occasional big dance. Or if the football or basketball teams received no athletic fees and no gate receipts, but instead depended on donations from grateful fans. What would be the result of these policies? A few top professors might eke out subsistence; universities would soon change their names to First National Bank of ———— as building after building was seized for nonpayment of due bonds; the football and basketball teams would become defunct.

Sporadic and uneven contributions, whether paid at registration or obtained from the proceeds of dances, concerts, or March of Dimes-like solicitations, cannot support major ongoing activities. They can't pay professors adequate salaries and they can't fund the activities of a Public Interest Research Group. Professionals may be willing to work at greatly reduced salaries in order to have the opportunity to serve the public interest. But few would be willing to risk their own or their families' welfare on the periodic gamble of a successful concert or a door-to-door solicitation. Besides, even the most ambitious periodic fund-raising schemes would be hard pressed to meet a budget such as the one set forth at the end of this chapter. Another important consideration is that the effort to promote these activities requires wasteful expenditures of time, energy, and money. Instead of pursuing their educations, students who wished to fund a PIRG in this fashion would be turned into mini-Madison Avenue hacks, spinning out a new promotion a week, each one wilder and more desperate than the last in a never-ending battle to raise money.

Universities have long realized that to obtain surety of income, they have to collect fees regularly on an "if you don't pay, you can't attend class or graduate" basis. This system is now under attack as more and more students realize that they have had no say in the imposition of student fees and, in the great majority of schools, no say in their disposition, either. Increasingly, students are demanding the right to allocate their activity and athletic fees and even to decide whether there should be any fees at all. But to acknowledge this long-overdue right is not to suggest that all activity fees are intrinsically evil or that no student-sponsored referendum or petition campaign, even if it garners overwhelming support, should be the basis for imposing a fee. On the contrary, the power to control student fees implies the right to raise as well as lower them.

Some students take the position that all activity fees should be abolished outright. This argument is easily understood when the thousands of dollars wasted each year by unresponsive newspapers and do-nothing student governments are tallied. The logic usually proceeds along the following lines: every student should be free to choose which activities to support; no one should be forced to pay a fee unwillingly; therefore all activity fees should be voluntary to insure that freedom of choice is maintained. The corollary of this argument is that if students really want an activity they will support it voluntarily. If they are not willing to do this, the activity should be abolished.

A more logical proposition is that student control of fees is what is needed. Such control would turn power over to the group that is paying the fee but leave students the right to raise, lower, or abolish fees. To hold to the proposition that all fees be abolished, regardless of student sentiment, is to take away all student rights. To hold to the other view, that all fees should be voluntary, regardless of student sentiment, is to elevate the principle of minority *rule* above any concept of community *rights*. This notion that the community has no rights, translated to a societal setting, cuts away at the roots of democracy. It elevates individualism to a sacrosanct position and leads inevitably to a form of contrived anarchy.

Ironically, when this line of reasoning is carried beyond the campus gates, only a few students or administrators give it credence. Submit the following propositions to a vote and overwhelming numbers of students would vote in the negative:

1. The rich should be free to support whatever they choose and to bequeath their entire fortunes to whomever they like without interference.
2. No person should be taxed to support welfare families, to give food to the hungry, or to maintain school systems.
3. Motel and restaurant owners should be permitted to serve whomever they please. No owner has to serve anyone he doesn't like.

The prescriptions that are denounced as reactionary or racist when applied to real-world events become elevated in the minds of a few students and many administrators to matters of moral principle when applied to the PIRG plan. Curiously, the compelling logic falters when a PIRG advocate asks an administrator whether the same principle of voluntarism can be applied to athletic fees.

One reason for the controversy surrounding fee payments is the confusion in many people's minds between minority *rights* and minority *rule.* If the former is observed, basic constitutional protections are accorded the minority, but the will of the majority in nonprotected areas prevails. The latter principle, minority *rule,* allows the few to frustrate the many, ignoring majority rights and the broader question of community control. For many, the image of the courageous minority is that of the lone draft resister fighting off the selective service bureaucracy. Or the image of Gene McCarthy and his few students in the snows of New Hampshire. These, of course, are examples of minorities exercising their rights. But there are other less romantic examples in which minority rights become minority rule. Consider the brave corporation shaping the tax code to preserve wealth for its shareholders at the expense of the public. Or the slum landlord preserving his prerogatives at the expense of his tenants. Minority status is no guarantee of a just cause, and if society—at large or on the campus—is to function at all, majority as well as minority rights must be protected.

The only resolution of these conflicts is to recognize that rights do conflict, but that so long as basic, constitutionally protected rights are not interfered with the majority must be given the heavier weight. There is no alternative.

One final aspect of this problem of wholly voluntary donations versus systematized collections should be examined. Not only is the fee debate taking place on the campus, it presently is raging in several state legislatures. However, these same arguments lose their philosophical gloss when they leave the campus and enter legislative chambers. "Fees are used to support pornography in the campus newspaper," thundered some New York State senators when they voted down all student fees. Fortunately, their colleagues in the House refused to go along. In other states the same blatant appeal to extreme right-wing myths is being used to justify abolition of all fees.

In future years, this struggle will emerge more clearly and be seen for what it is, a battle between those who wish to curtail all student activities save sports and the three R's and those who believe students have the right to associate freely, publish their own newspapers, elect their own student officers, and hire their own PIRG professionals. In many ways, those legislators who are trying to eliminate all fees are more clever than many of their student allies who think that the campaign will save their money and eliminate useless student governments. These legislators know that without fees students cannot support long-term, ongoing activities. Their aim is to remove the tools of student activism, and by so doing they hope that campus apathy will deepen and harden into an immovable barrier to prevent any resurgence of student energy.

MANDATORY FEES

Most campuses presently have mandatory fee systems to support all campus activities. Mandatory fees eliminate the need for fund-raising campaigns and provide great financial stability, but they are shamelessly coercive and leave the student with one of two choices: pay or leave. Viewed strictly in financial terms, a mandatory payment guarantees collection and eliminates the need for student fund-raising campaigns. Unfortunately, it also eliminates all individual rights as well as the right of the student body acting collectively to change the fee structure. Moreover, it enables the organizers of student activities to grow fat and unresponsive, since they are completely unaccountable to their student constituencies. Whether or not they perform satisfactorily, fees will still come pouring in. Because responsiveness and accountability are the philosophical underpinnings of the PIRG proposal, mandatory fees by themselves are unacceptable as a means of support for a PIRG.

ALTERNATIVE FEE SYSTEMS

Between the extremes of wholly voluntary donations and mandatory fees are a number of alternative systems. Each of these strikes a different balance between the legitimate rights of the student community and the rights of its individual members. The present mandatory fee system, for example, gives no rights to individuals, while the substitution of a voluntary fee system, unless approved by a student majority, eliminates the rights of the student community as a whole. Of course, the impact of each of these systems can be moderated by permitting periodic referendums to decide whether or not to retain a particular fee system. Probably the fairest way to guarantee both community and individual rights would be to maintain community-wide fee collection but institute a mechanism whereby any student who chose not to pay a particular fee would still be permitted to attend class and graduate. This last alternative is the best way to fund a Public Interest Research Group, since it preserves a student's freedom while providing the necessary stability to insure the PIRG's continuance.

There are two ways this collection method can operate: by a negative checkoff or by a mandatory payment with a guaranteed refund.

1. A negative checkoff system permits each student at registration to choose not to participate in the PIRG plan by filling out a special form to *avoid* the fee payment. In effect, this system permits each student to decide at each registration period whether to participate in the PIRG plan.

Obviously, a negative checkoff system works best when all activities, or at least all activities of a particular type, utilize it. If PIRG is the only activity subject to this "registration referendum," it is at a serious disadvantage, since large numbers of students may express their resentment at fees in general by withdrawing the PIRG fee. But there are even more serious flaws to this system. Most important, a PIRG is incapable of operating if its financial base is in jeopardy two or three times a year. Second, this system takes away all majority rights. If the majority of the student body or the majority of those voting in an approved election vote to implement the PIRG as a campus activity, their votes are made worthless if, each time there is a new registration period, a new referendum in effect is carried out. Third, it places freshmen and transfer students in an unfair position. These newcomers are forced to make an on-the-spot decision as to whether they wish to support an activity they have never heard of, know nothing about, and cannot evaluate. A few posters or information brochures at registration cannot supply all the answers to the questions of bewildered first registrants.

Because of these disadvantages the negative checkoff is only slightly better than voluntary or mandatory collections. Fortunately, there is another alternative.

2. A mandatory fee increase with a guaranteed refund avoids the problems of the negative checkoff system. It is always difficult to ascribe boundaries to the concept of student rights. How much power should students have over the governance of the university, over faculty tenure decisions, or over what stocks make up the endowment portfolio? These are subtle questions and reasonable people can come to different conclusions. But it is difficult to imagine student rights having any meaning whatsoever unless students at least have the power to determine which student fees are to be assessed and how they are to be collected and disposed of. In the case of the PIRG plan, it seems clear that if a majority agreement can be reached concerning one or another fee system, and if that system protects basic student rights, the majority of students should be allowed to establish their own collection program. Of course, there are limits to majority rule set by the university charter and state and federal law. But within those bounds, students should be given self-determination.

The mandatory fee with a guaranteed refund operates in the following way: First, a majority (or plurality) of the student body indicates by petition or ballot (see next section) that it wishes to form a Public Interest Research Group and fund it with a fee increase. Second, the student body presents this proposal to the appropriate administrative board. Third, the collection plan, if approved, with its refund provision, is put into effect at the next registration period.

36

THE MEANS

At registration, the PIRG fee is collected in the same way as any other fee: by the registrar's office. All the money, except for university collection costs, is then turned over to the PIRG. The PIRG holds the money until the third or fourth week of the school term, when refunds are given to students who do not wish to be part of the PIRG plan. This right to obtain the total fee collection and hold it for three weeks, during which time the majority who support the PIRG can attempt to win over the minority who oppose it or the apathetic who may ignore it, is the basic right obtained by the successful petition drive or referendum.

There are numerous advantages to this fee system which make it superior to voluntary, mandatory, or negative checkoff arrangements. Because the collection process is organized and regular it is inherently more stable than a wholly voluntary donation, even though each student voluntarily chooses whether to support the PIRG. Because the plan is predicated on obtaining majority student approval, it is far more democratic than a straight mandatory system. In addition, the refund provision serves to protect the rights of each individual student at every registration period.

Of course, this funding system—and, for that matter, any other organized system—places a burden on dissenters. In this case they have to take the trouble to go and collect their refunds. But this slight burden has to be weighed against the majority right to determine its own collection procedures. At worst, a dissenting student would have to spend a few minutes of one day each term to obtain a refund. This burden can be further reduced by placing the refund office in a convenient location and by requiring extensive notice of the refund period to be given by posters, newspaper ads, and announcements on campus radio or television.

The real question underlying much of the debate that occurred during the 1971–72 academic year is whether a majority *ever* has the right to impose demands, however slight, on the minority. Anyone who believes in rule by law has to answer this question in the affirmative. The alternative is to endorse a utopian concept of peaceful anarchy. In the setting of the campus, if majority student votes are not going to be heeded concerning support for a PIRG, the only option is a return to rule by administration fiat, a concept discarded painfully at most schools during the mid-1960's.

Once the question of the fee collection mechanism is decided a decision must be made concerning the best way to obtain student approval. There are two ways a student body can endorse the PIRG plan: petition or referendum.

Petition or Referendum?

Either a petition drive or a referendum can determine student support for the PIRG plan; a petition drive is the better way, especially at large universities. Experience shows that on most campuses fewer than 25 percent of the eligible voters participate in referendums. Theoretically, a referendum attracting only a handful of students could impose a fee increase on all students. Of course, the same procedure could be used to reverse the original positive vote.

By contrast, a petition drive that yields signatures from a majority of the campus insures that at least half the campus has been exposed to the PIRG concept. The dialogue that takes place between petitioners and students allows the PIRG idea to be sharpened as well as giving opponents the opportunity to gather support for their own views. To obtain support from a majority of the student body requires the efforts of hundreds of dedicated petitioners.

At some schools, however, students have the power to regulate all student fees through referendum. If this is the already accepted procedure for instituting new fees, there is no reason to switch to a petition drive despite its many positive points.

38

THE MEANS

At some schools where no formal procedures exist for student control over fees, administrators have refused to give weight to signed petitions. The board of governors of Rutgers University, for example, ignored the signed support of thousands of Rutgers students and required the PIRG organizers to hold a referendum. They did, and the referendum was overwhelmingly approved, whereupon NJPIRG was established. Similar situations occurred at other campuses and PIRG organizers were forced to sponsor referendums *after* they had already collected the signatures of a majority of the student body.

Future PIRG organizers should take this antipetition policy by administrators into account. One obvious course of action is both to petition and to conduct a referendum. If students have the power to raise their own fees, they can follow the example of Syracuse University, Michigan State, and Boston College students who obtained signatures from a large number, but not a majority, of students, and then, following the approved procedures of their schools, adopted the PIRG proposal by binding referendums. In the final analysis the choice between conducting a petition drive or holding a referendum must be left to each participating campus.

Fee Increase

The last decision to be made before the PIRG organizing drive begins concerns the fee increase. The amount should not be so large as to constitute a burden on poorer students nor so small that it can't support the PIRG. Most schools which have approved the plan so far have increased fees by $1.00 per student per quarter or $2.00 per student per semester. A few have raised fees by only $1.50 per semester, and schools in Vermont, where the student population is small, have increased fees by $3.00 per student per semester. For the vast majority of students these amounts are so trivial as to pass unnoticed. Considering the

PIRG: A MODEL BUDGET

(Estimated operating expenses for one fiscal year for a PIRG with support base of between fifty thousand and sixty thousand students. This model may be expanded or reduced to fit different size student bases.)

A. EMPLOYEE COSTS

10	Professionals (for example, 9 professionals—$7,500.00; 1 executive director—$10,500.00)	$ 78,000.00
3	Secretarial and clerical employees (for example, 1 administrative secretary—$650.00 per month; 2 secretaries—$500.00 per month)	19,800.00
2	Full-time equivalent community workers—$6,000 each	12,000.00
		$ 109,800.00
	Employee benefits	12,700.00
	Total Employee Costs	$ 122,500.00

B. OCCUPANCY COSTS

	Space rental (2,100 sq. ft. at $4.50 per sq. ft. per year)	$ 9,450.00
	Electricity—$40.00 per month	480.00
	Total Occupancy Costs	$ 9,930.00

C. OFFICE EQUIPMENT

4	Electric typewriters—$390.00 each	$ 1,560.00
14	Desks and chairs (for example, 10 desks and swivel armchairs at $210.00 each; 4 secretarial desks and chairs at $240.00 each)	3,060.00
24	Side chairs—$30.00 each	720.00
8	File cabinets—4-drawer	
	3 legal-size—$95.00 each	285.00
	5 letter-size—$85.00 each	425.00
10	Book shelves—$95.00 each	950.00
	Total Equipment Costs	$ 7,000.00

Typewriter maintenance—$42.00 per machine
Equipment cost amortized over 10 years $ 700.00
168.00

Total Equipment Cost per year $ 868.00

D. *CONTINGENCY FUND*
Includes cost of books and legal publications, projected litigation costs $ 7,500.00

E. *OFFICE COSTS*
Consumable supplies—$200.00 per person X 14 $ 2,800.00
Telephone:
Key-type switchboard—$250.00 per month (5 lines plus intercom) 3,000.00
Long-distance calls—$7.50 per day X 240 1,800.00
Postage—40 mailings per day X 240 768.00
Duplicating costs—$100.00 per month (machine rental and use) 1,200.00

Total Office Costs $ 9,568.00

F. *STUDENT RESEARCH PROJECTS*
For example, 15–20 summer projects, grants of approximately $1,000.00 each, to cover equipment, operating expenses, and minimal wages. $ 20,000.00

G. *CITIZEN ORGANIZING* $ 10,000.00

H. *PUBLIC EDUCATION*
Includes cost of publishing PIRG reports, advertising, and other publicity $ 15,000.00

I. *CERTIFIED PUBLIC ACCOUNTANT*
Annual audit of PIRG financial records $ 500.00

TOTAL ANNUAL OPERATING EXPENSES $ 195,866.00

money spent by students on beer, wine, cigarettes, candies, soft drinks, and the like, an annual $3.00 or $4.00 fee, amounting to around a penny a day, is dwarfed into insignificance.

Although each individual contribution is minimal, the aggregate is large enough to fund a Public Interest Research Group. For example, if fifty thousand students from seven schools participate and pay $2.00 per semester, $200,000, less refunds, would be collected. Considering the operating costs of a PIRG, this sum is not unreasonably large. Salaries for the professionals, office equipment, and student wages are necessary expenses. Of course if fewer students participate, the group can be scaled down accordingly.

The budget on the preceding pages illustrates the major expenses.

3 THE STRUCTURE OF THE PUBLIC INTEREST RESEARCH GROUP

The vague notion of a PIRG advocating student concerns must be translated into the realities of a functioning organization composed of a dozen or more schools and twenty-five thousand to one hundred thousand students. Student PIRG organizations cannot leave to chance the spirit of cooperation that will unite the campuses into a functioning body. They must plan the campus and intercampus structure of the organization before the PIRG concept is publicized or student approval sought. They must clearly delineate lines of authority and control to insure fair representation and to avoid needless misunderstanding and antagonism. Obviously, no final plan can be adopted until all participating schools have passed the proposal and elected student boards of directors. But a clear idea of organization should be formulated at the outset.

The precise form of organization may vary from group to group but the following model should apply in most cases.

Overview

On each campus where the PIRG concept receives student and administrative approval, students elect representatives for local boards of directors. In turn, each local board selects one or more of its members to represent it on a state board. The state board consists of local board representatives from all participating colleges and universities.*

The large number of students involved and the geographical diversity of participating schools necessitate this kind of structure for student representation. There is no practical way for tens of thousands of students, separated by hundreds of miles, to vote individually on each proposed activity of the group. Nor is it possible for any meaningful communication to occur between the professional staff and such large numbers of students, except through representative boards.

Even to include all local board members on a state board is unfeasible. In Minnesota, for example, over one hundred students serve on local boards at twenty participating universities. Such a large group meeting once or twice a month would be prohibitively expensive. Therefore the best solution to insure representative control is to set up a tiered system which allows power to flow from the student bodies at large through local and state boards to the professional staff.

The Local Boards

Local boards of directors elected by students on each participating campus are the most important component of the PIRG structure. More than any other factor, the activities of the local board will shape the image of the PIRG in the minds of students. The professional staff, by necessity, is removed from most campuses in the state. The staff is able to provide continuity and expertise, generate occasional news stories, and make its influence felt on the state legislature and state agencies. But the professional

---

* Representation on the state board should be proportioned to the number of contributing students at the various schools. See Table I.

TABLE I

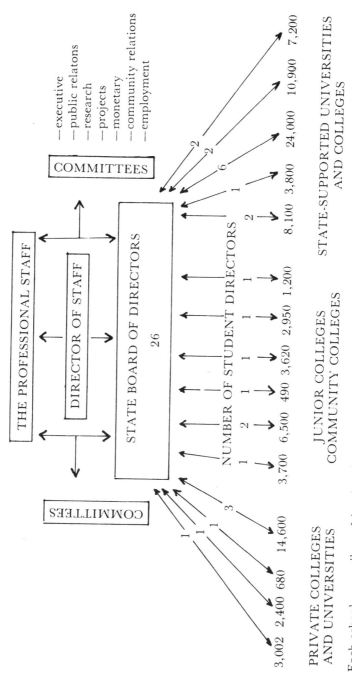

THE PROFESSIONAL STAFF

DIRECTOR OF STAFF

STATE BOARD OF DIRECTORS
26

COMMITTEES

COMMITTEES

NUMBER OF STUDENT DIRECTORS

—executive
—public relatons
—research
—projects
—monetary
—community relations
—employment

STATE-SUPPORTED UNIVERSITIES
AND COLLEGES

2   2   6   1

7,200   10,900   24,000   3,800

8,100

2

JUNIOR COLLEGES
COMMUNITY COLLEGES

1   1   1

1,200   2,950   3,620

1

490

1   2   1

6,500   3,700

PRIVATE COLLEGES
AND UNIVERSITIES

3   1   1   1

14,600   680   2,400   3,002

Each school, regardless of its size, is entitled to at least one member on the board of directors. However, for every four thousand students above the first four thousand, each school is entitled to an additional member on the board.

staff can't begin to deal with the problems which crop up on the local level. Only PIRG chapters on each campus can do this. The state board is in the same position as the professional staff. Its focus must be to assume an overview of state operations. It cannot deeply involve itself with community concerns.

If the PIRG is to make its presence felt on each campus and in town and city councils, the local board must provide the means. Therefore, the success or failure of local PIRG projects will be measured by the strength or weakness of the local board on each campus.

SIZE

The size of the university usually will determine the number of representatives serving on the local board of directors. To perform all of the duties of a local board, however, no fewer than five directors are needed. For the sake of efficiency, the board should not exceed twenty-five even at the largest schools.

ELECTION OF BOARD MEMBERS

Depending on the size and traditions of the university, board members may be selected in one campus-wide election or by a series of elections held in the various schools of the university. Small schools probably should hold a single campus-wide election while major universities with graduate and professional schools may require separate elections in each school. The number of representatives each school in the university elects should be proportional to the number of students enrolled in the school.

STRUCTURE OF THE LOCAL BOARD

Individual board members cannot hope to have the time to be familiar with each issue brought before the board. Because these issues are complex and cover broad areas of procedural and substantive knowledge, the only practical way for the board to function is on a committee system. Each local board should have consumer, environment, equal opportunity, and government affairs committees to cover substantive areas, and publicity and coordination committees in the procedural area. Larger boards can specialize further and have air and water pollution committees, a tax reform committee, and committees studying other specialized problems of particular interest to the group, which may not fit under other categories.

Each committee should consist of two or three board members and, if possible, a nonvoting adviser expert in the subject area. An effort should be made to include community residents as well as faculty members as advisers. Committee members must perform several functions. First they must screen and evaluate projects submitted by students, faculty, and community residents. Second, they must keep abreast of professional staff activities in their respective subject areas. Third, they should seek to persuade faculty members to offer credit courses or independent study credits (on the increase generally) in areas suitable for PIRG involvement. But the most important function of local board committees is to generate community projects suitable for action by students or mixed teams of students and professional staff members. The local board is not a mini-foundation that placidly sits back and waits for projects to be suggested by others. On the contrary, it should constantly be fashioning its own activities to guarantee broad student participation, even if no student independently suggests a project. At the same time it must not become so internally energetic that it discourages participation by non-board members.*

In order to carry out their tasks, student board members

---

* To discourage this type of clannishness, state board members should be prohibited from participating in substantive projects. The same prohibition probably should apply to local board chair persons.

must possess or develop some expertise in a subject area. This means that they must be prepared to study the area for which they have responsibility. Local boards should maintain small libraries and subscribe to a few periodicals in the subject areas in which they are active. One excellent way to encourage study by committee members is to arrange academic credit for independent study in the subject field of their responsibility. In this way board members can reduce their course loads while receiving an incentive for becoming better PIRG directors.

LOCAL BOARD PROJECTS

An effective local board should aggressively undertake projects of its own and mobilize campus resources to carry out projects suggested by the state board and the professional staff. In addition, the local board should be concerned with the immediate needs of students. For example, every major school participating in the PIRG should establish a consumer action center (see Chapter 9) to help student and community residents with individual consumer complaints. Similarly the board can set up an automobile safety and complaint center, a tenant's union, a local lobby to monitor the town or city council, and task forces to carry out action projects having local significance, such as retail price comparisons. The local board also should arrange to have credit courses offered to disseminate consumer or environmental information and to provide interested students with a vehicle to carry out empirical research on local problems. Of course all local projects should be coordinated with the state board to avoid conflicts or duplication of effort.

STATE BOARD RELATIONS

An important duty of the local board is to express the concerns of its constituents to the state board. To do this well, the board should hold regular public meetings at which students, faculty, and members of the community can present proposals and hear reports on the activities of the professional staff. The local board should serve as a clearinghouse for local projects, screening them, carrying out preliminary investigations, and, if necessary, recommending appropriate action by the state board or professional staff. A campus office, a well-publicized phone number and post office box, regular columns in the campus press, and distribution of a PIRG newsletter also help to keep communication channels open.

COMMUNITY RELATIONS

Another duty of local boards (and the state board, as well) is to coordinate their activities with ongoing projects sponsored by community groups. It is wasteful, for instance, to begin a water pollution study if a citizen group is already acting effectively on the problem. Resources are scarce and the PIRG should concentrate on areas which are not being serviced by other citizen representatives.

A local board can strengthen itself enormously by appealing to community residents for help and by offering help to groups in need of student or professional aid. Also there are ways that residents in the community can aid the PIRG. In most communities permanent or semipermanent volunteers can be found to staff an office and help build ties to the community. High school students and other younger students in the community can often participate in PIRG projects. In Minnesota, a group of girl scouts did much of the survey work necessary for MPIRG's retail price comparison in local grocery stores.*

---

* Vermont organizers carried this idea a step further. They've included high school students and community residents on local boards and permitted groups of 200 nonuniversity citizens to contribute $1,200 ($6 per person per year, the standard VPIRG fee), and become a local VPIRG group with their own local board and the right to elect a representative to the state board.

49

The State Board

Each local board elects representatives to the state board from among its own members. Every college or university gets at least one seat, with additional seats distributed on a proportionate basis. For example, in Minnesota, for every five thousand students above an initial five thousand, schools receive an additional seat on the state board. Thus, with eighteen hundred students, Carleton College has one seat, Mankato State College, with twelve thousand students, has two seats, and the Minneapolis campus of the University of Minnesota, with forty-one thousand five hundred students, has eight seats.

DUTIES OF THE STATE BOARD

The state board is charged with coordinating local board activities, building statewide alliances with other citizen groups, and, if circumstances require it, initiating projects on a multi-state basis with other PIRG groups. The primary duties of the state board are to determine overall strategy and to select priorities for research and action. To carry out these duties effectively, state board members, even more than their counterparts on the local board level, must achieve sophistication in a variety of subject areas. It is incumbent upon each state director to become familiar in a general fashion with the field of public interest advocacy and to develop a relatively high degree of specialization in one particular issue area. To facilitate this, the state board should follow the same pattern as local boards and divide into procedural and substantive committees. However, on the state level two new committees must be formed that will greatly influence the work of the PIRG. The first of these, the employment committee, is responsible for recruiting and hiring the professional staff. The second is an executive committee with power to authorize staff action in interim periods between meetings of the full board. Other committees may be formed if more specialized expertise is needed.

PIRG STRUCTURE

No formula has yet been developed to fix the precise relationships between the staff and the state board. As a result, each of the existing PIRGs has passed through several major alterations in staff-board relations. In general, the state board should determine overall strategy, leaving tactical decisions to the professional staff. Unfortunately, while clear in concept, this neat distinction has proved difficult to apply in practice.

However, some important lessons have been learned from the experiences of the first PIRGs. Because students are the employers and the professional staff the employees of the PIRG, the student board always retains full authority and has the final say. But the board must exercise its power discreetly. Lawyers and scientists will not be able to work effectively, if at all, for a student group whose actions prove arbitrary and capricious. The need for student control must balance against the professional's need for independence and freedom of action on a day-to-day basis. It is the responsibility of the student board to define this relationship as clearly as possible so that indecision and doubt do not hamstring action.

The director of the professional staff must be given *real* authority by the student board or else the title becomes a label without meaning. The director should be the only professional to meet with the state board of student directors on a regular basis. The requests of the state board should be conveyed to individual professionals by the director, who also should be responsible for approving (or rejecting) the work produced by staff members.

Any interstaff problems should be handled by the director and the board acting together. Except in the most unusual circumstances, there should be no ex parte meetings between the staff and the student board. Such meetings are bound to divide the staff into competing factions, with individual members jockey-

51

ing for student board approval. The importance of avoiding this type of game playing and power tripping can't be overemphasized. If it isn't kept under control, it is the surest way to render the PIRG ineffective.

Finally, the state board has to resist steadfastly a tendency to endlessly discuss ultimate goals and various types of interpersonal relationships. The student bull session is a venerable institution with a long, if somewhat checkered, tradition. When transferred to a PIRG, it becomes terribly counterproductive. Of course, concerns over style and interpersonal dealings are important, but relationships and goals are best defined by aggressive action—not interminable discussion. A truly effective group will work out relationships as a by-product of its other work. To center on these problems is to cripple the PIRG's action stance and to reduce it to a very expensive encounter group.

The Professional Staff

Because the staff consists of professionals with expertise in a variety of subject areas, there are many possibilities for action and many forms that action can take. Obviously the first step in any project is research. Depending on the project, this may be undertaken by a member of the professional staff, by student research groups, by student-faculty groups (in some cases it might be appropriate to make research part of a regular course or seminar), or by other task forces. On the basis of this research the professional staff recommends action to the state board.

If the recommendation is approved, the staff director assigns a professional to proceed with the project. The gravity and urgency of the problem determines the appropriate response. Ordinarily, the staff pursues a gradually escalating series of tactics. One or more—fact-finding, persuasion, public education, and

---

TABLE II
OUTLINE OF PIRG STRUCTURE

Duties of the Local Board
1. Serve as a link between students and the state board.
2. Mobilize campus resources to work on projects organized by the professional staff.
3. Supervise projects of its own design.
4. Cooperate with other campus and community groups.
5. Elect and, if necessary, recall representatives to the state board.

Duties of the State Board
1. Determine priority areas for professional staff action.
2. Supervise the activities of the local boards.
3. Coordinate PIRG projects with other state or national public interest groups.
4. Assume responsibility for all financial and administrative details pertaining to the professional staff.
5. Serve as the official spokesman of the group.

Activities of the Professional Staff
1. Implement the decisions of the state board.
2. Supervise student/faculty research teams.
3. Engage in research, investigations, public education, lobbying, and litigation.

---

lobbying—usually precede litigation.*

The professional staff has an important duty to assist students with local projects. These projects may not be as important or as glamorous as statewide actions. They may even be considered draining in that they tend to eat up valuable staff time. But it must be remembered that one important function of the PIRG plan is citizenship training at the local level.

---

* See Table II.

Staff members should establish close ties with other citizen groups active in the state. Ordinarily, to the surprise of many students, the PIRG will be larger, be better funded, and have more resources than any other citizen-supported organization. This permits the PIRG staff to serve as a catalyst and weld together coalitions of concerned citizens to work on particular issues. The respectability and added strength of these community groups can greatly increase the PIRG's effectiveness, while the PIRG's resources, such as full-time professionals, student manpower, and a firm funding base, serve as a valuable complement to existing community groups which share the PIRG's concerns.

The Legal Structure

The PIRG should be set up as a nonprofit, tax-exempt corporation. (See Chapter 7 for discussion about tax questions.) This corporation is a separate legal entity, distinct from each of the participating schools. Students elect a student board of directors, and the board appoints or elects the officers of the corporation. These officers are usually members of the student board.

The corporation has to establish binding legal contracts with participating schools setting forth the rights and obligations of each. In general, the contract is not very different from that signed by any other independent corporation doing business with the university. The agreement is an arm's-length relation, giving each party the right to enforce the other's performance. Basically, the PIRG agrees to take part in (or refrain from) certain activities in consideration for the fee per student per quarter or per semester. Similarly, the university agrees to serve as a collecting agent for the PIRG.*

* See Appendix 2 for sample PIRG contracts.

4 THE HISTORY OF THE FIRST STUDENT PIRGS

The original idea for Public Interest Research Groups was developed during the summer and fall of 1970. The essence of the proposal was that students tax themselves a nominal sum in order to hire advocates to seek creative solutions to public interest problems. However, long before the specifics of this proposal were formulated, it had become apparent that there was a critical need for new public interest professionals to work on the state and local level. The handful of Washington lawyers and scientists working in the public interest arena do not have the resources and, in some cases, the expertise, to deal with complicated local issues. On the other hand, most citizen groups are not able to hire even a single full-time staff member, let alone several attorneys and scientists. Consequently, many battles have been lost by default.

This lack of citizen power has been complicated and made more harmful by the fact that states are dominated by special interest group representatives, and most state agencies which had been set up to license and regulate on behalf of the public interest have abdicated their statutory roles completely. As a result, citizens are left unprotected by government and without the means to control substantially their own destinies. The results of this imbalance of power can be seen in the long absence of strong consumer and environmental legislation, understaffed state agencies that don't have the resources to enforce the legislation that does exist, massive property tax breaks and other privileges given to large industries, and a long list of similar complaints which share the same characteristic disregard of citizen well-being.

At the same time, hundreds of new graduates are seeking to harmonize their ideals with their work by finding employment in the public service area. During the 1970–71 academic year, seven hundred young professionals applied for work with Ralph Nader's Public Interest Research Group even though the salary was only $4,500 per year. There were openings for only nine. A few were able to locate other public interest jobs, but for the majority there simply were no positions available. One important incentive behind the PIRG plan was the desire to increase the opportunities for public interest work so as not to waste the idealism, talent, and energy of committed professionals.

Various types of proposals were studied before the PIRG model was chosen. The first suggestion examined called for harnessing in a systematic fashion the part-time talent of professionals associated with private firms or industry. There were several serious weaknesses with this proposal, starting with the fact that while many law firms, for example, are willing to permit their associates to handle indigent criminal or civil cases, few are anxious to allow their lawyers to get involved in major public policy disputes. Also, a shifting collection of volunteers is too unstable a base on which to build a public interest group. Volunteers from private firms, for instance, would never be able to build up expertise in public interest areas, such as air and water pollution, unless their regular jobs dealt with those problems. If they did, conflicts of interest probably would prevent volunteers from taking such cases. No oil company attorney, to cite an obvious example, would be permitted to take the Alaska pipeline case even if his company owned no north-shore leases. Also, major cases involve major commitments of time, not the few hours per day or per month that most volunteers can spare. For these and other reasons, it was felt that pro bono volunteers would best be used to supplement and back up the efforts of a full-time staff.

The second model studied involved the use of law, medical, and science students. Their work in the public interest would be integrated into their regular clinical curricula. However, this type of firm would marshal limited expertise and provide no continuity, since it would be founded on a base that is by definition unstable. Like the assistance of part-time volunteers, the work of students would be a welcome addition to the efforts of the regular staff, but neither could replace the full-time staff.

The only proposal which seemed to answer all expectations was to form on the local level the same type of groups that already existed in Washington, D.C. Unfortunately, the reality of the situation was that the Washington firms themselves were already extended to their limits and had neither the manpower nor the finances to establish local affiliates. Foundation funding was impractical because foundations could provide enough money to start only a handful of demonstration firms and most foundations were already fully committed. Besides, foundation money almost always has a two- or three-year time limit. At the end of that period new sources of support must be located. Also, most foundation grants are held to specific projects and other conditions and not suitable for the unrestricted actions of a public interest group. Another possibility was to tap the resources of individual large donors. But only a very few private individuals are willing or able to turn $150,000 or more over to as novel an organization as a public interest firm.

In a few large cities public interest firms can partly support themselves by charging fees, but most by necessity are small in size and their work is mostly limited to clients who can afford to pay or cases which can produce fees. Rather than depend on the short-term contributions of foundations and philanthropists or settle for a small litigation-oriented firm, it was decided to form groups of professionals with a wider and more permanent financial base. The decision was made to construct the PIRG on the foundation of a citizen support base. The first effort in this area needed a distinct segment of the citizenry whose own self-interest would be served by the group's formation.

Students seemed an obvious choice to fill this prescription. In the first place they were among the most severe critics of present-day society. Second, they could provide a great deal more than funding. Their energy could be turned into public interest activities and the part-time efforts of students could provide a strong backup to the work of the full-time staff. Third, the PIRG would benefit students by increasing the range of clinical courses offered and by permitting their research to be integrated into the regular academic curriculum. The PIRG proposal offered students the opportunity to tie social concern and activism to academic credit. It could also serve to interest them in the idea and necessity of full-time citizenship career roles after graduation.* For such reasons it was decided to entrust the PIRG proposal to students.

During September and October 1970, Nader and four of his associates visited over forty campuses proposing the plan. By the end of the academic year, students in many states across the country had responded. Students in Oregon and Minnesota were first. Interested students in both states formed organizing committees, publicized the plan, and held petition drives and referendums to gauge the extent of student support. In Oregon, all seven schools in the state college system approved a proposition to create the

* For a perspective on the effect of PIRGs on Alumni, see "Student Public Interest Research Groups (PIRGs): Educational Internships for Responsible Active Citizenship," by Professor Samuel M. Loescher, *Indiana Business Review*, August-September 1972.

HISTORY OF THE FIRST PIRGS

Oregon Student Public Interest Research Group (OSPIRG). Several private schools and community colleges also joined in the plan. At the University of Minnesota, in less than two weeks, student PIRG organizers obtained signatures of support from more than 60 percent of the forty-two-thousand-member student body. Other state-supported and private universities registered equally impressive totals. By the end of the spring quarter, over fifty thousand students had registered support for the Minnesota Public Interest Research Group (MPIRG). Both states received the approval of their boards of trustees during the spring of 1971.

The Growth in PIRGs, 1971–72

The MPIRG and OSPIRG efforts provided models for the first edition of this manual. In general, their experiences were repeated in state after state during the 1971–72 academic year, when twelve new PIRGs were formed. In the fall of 1971, Vermont became the third state to form a PIRG. The entire VPIRG campaign took only six weeks. During this time about 60 percent of the students in the state enrolled in VPIRG and students at the University of Vermont secured the unanimous approval of the plan by the Board of Regents. Other boards of regents, in New Jersey, Iowa, Massachusetts, and Michigan, have also approved the establishment of PIRG groups at state-supported schools. Several state attorney generals have rendered opinions favorable to the PIRG program. Excerpts from an opinion by J. Shane Creamer, attorney general of Pennsylvania, are contained in Appendix 3.

Leading private schools in many states have also adopted the PIRG proposal. Among these are Syracuse University (CNYPIRG), Boston College (MassPIRG East), Williams College (Western MassPIRG), Duke University and St. Andrews College (NCPIRG), Rice University (TexPIRG), and St. Louis and Washington Universities (MOPIRG). The complete list of new PIRG groups is contained in Appendix 1.

Not all attempts to form PIRGs have been equally successful. The most common cause of failure is lack of organization on the part of student proponents of PIRGs. In some cases a small clique takes over the effort and drives away potential support because of its introverted exclusivity. In other cases, student organizers become overanxious and attempt to begin work on substantive projects before they have finished organizing their schools. Invariably, this course spells disaster, and while a few projects may be completed successfully, no ongoing effort remains when the year ends. Sometimes after successfully securing student approval and winning endorsements from faculty members and community leaders, the proposal is rejected by regents or trustees. Indiana University, for example, built the largest base of student and community support any student organization had ever achieved, but Chancellor Carter opposed the plan stating he "could see no reason to adopt it." In the states of Washington and Pennsylvania, individual trustees blackmailed universities by threatening to resign if the PIRG were approved. These primitive tactics can delay final implementation of the PIRG plan but they can't prevent it entirely. The student vote and the coming unionization of the campuses eventually will sweep out trustees whose paleolithic views prevent the practice of responsible citizenship.

Ironically, the opponents of PIRG often were the same officials who a few years before had urged students not to demonstrate or sit in but to work peacefully within the system. Now when students attempted to follow this advice the rules of the game were changed. It is worth analyzing the main objections to the PIRG plan.

For some administrators the issue revolves around control. "A PIRG can't use the university collection mechanism unless the university [read "administrators"] control it." But these same administrators deny they control student government or the school newspaper and they certainly do not control the health insurance plan or food services, which also use the collection processes of the university. Somehow a PIRG is different.

Chief among the administrators' objections seems to be a feeling that an increase in student activity fees, even if approved by an overwhelming majority of students, and even if refunds are freely offered, is unfair to those students who oppose the increase. These administrators become ardent libertarians when it comes to a PIRG fee: "If even one student out of a thousand doesn't wish to pay, his rights should be protected." This fear of minority coercion may be consistent at least, despite a majority vote, at schools where all activities are supported by voluntary donations. But even at these schools the student community should have the right to determine the means by which it chooses to support its own activities. At schools where a mandatory fee system, not voted on by students, supports activities which offer no refunds, this fear appears more a matter of hypocrisy, antagonism, or personal whim than a deep-seated belief. President Edward Bloustein of Rutgers University echoed the words of the many administrators who support the PIRG proposal. President Bloustein said that he thought students should be allowed to tax themselves if they want to for a project like PIRG. "Activities like skiing and chess club are funded out of student activity fees. They have less of an integral relation to education than this [PIRG]."

Another tactic employed by these administrators is to express approval for the concept of a PIRG but to oppose an orderly collection of fees. Unfortunately, the two are inextricable. The fee mechanism is necessary to provide stability while the refund option offers complete protection to dissenters. If all fees were voluntary, a PIRG would be able to hold its own in the competition for student activity funds. But if the competition is between mandatory fees and wholly voluntary donations, a voluntarily funded

PIRG or any other voluntarily supported activity is placed at a very serious disadvantage.

Beneath the stated objections to the PIRG fee may lurk another inarticulated fear. The PIRG fee raises the spectre of student control over the activity fee structure, a proposal some administrators fear and are at present trying to eliminate. For years student governments controlled only a small portion of the student activity fees. But in recent years the amount of discretionary money available to students has increased, so that in some cases students control hundreds of thousands of dollars. The reaction against this situation has been predictable. In several states, universities are under attack in the courts by ad hoc coalitions of student and community extremists to ban all student fees. They argue that no student should be forced to pay for an activity he or she doesn't support.

Many administrators favor a reduction in, or the elimination of, student fees. They know that when fees are eliminated, so will be the basis for organized student action. Without fee support, activities offices, with their typewriters, phones, and mimeograph machines, must close; many campus newspapers also will have to cease publication; and with the elimination of these resources will come the elimination of much student activism.

Thus far, boards of regents in three states have refused to approve the PIRG plan. The Texas board, led by the noted foe of student rights Frank Erwin, voted five to four not to approve TexPIRG at the University of Texas, Austin Campus. TexPIRG organizers, however, successfully passed petitions at other schools, and at the University of Texas an appeal for contributions brought in $25,000. The students plan to raise the PIRG question with the board again next year. INPIRG in Indiana was voted down by trustees at Indiana University, although Notre Dame University approved the program. Regents at the University of

Pittsburgh also vetoed the plan but did so during the summer vacation and as yet have given no reasons for their action. In view of the mounting string of endorsements from congressmen, senators, and governors, and the growing number of schools participating in the PIRG plan, these three vetoes seem to be aberrations which, it is hoped, will not be so easily repeated.

While new PIRGs were being formed, MPIRG and OSPIRG underwent rough first years. Although both received administrative approval in the spring of 1971, neither had sufficient funds to hire permanent staff until late in the summer. The four-month delay proved costly. Exhaustion engendered by the organizing effort and the fight for administrative approval caused a general letdown. Student enthusiasm declined markedly, a number of key organizers dropped out entirely, and little preparation was undertaken for the new school year. Consequently, when classes resumed in September some schools had to rebuild their organizations from the ground up. Others were left with small numbers of eager but inexperienced students. Only a few schools in each state had strong local boards prepared to begin work when class resumed in the new year.

OSPIRG suffered more, because most of the original PIRG organizers were seniors and graduation opened a temporary leadership vacuum. As a result of OSPIRG's slow start, refund levels soared to 25 percent at Oregon State University. By comparison, in Minnesota, no school utilizing the same funding mechanism recorded more than a 5 percent refund rate. Also, the level of MPIRG refunds dropped noticeably during the winter and spring quarters once the group had begun to work efficiently. This pattern seems to indicate that the rate of refunds in schools with a mandatory payment and guaranteed refund is a reliable indicator of student support. That is, refunds will rise or fall in accordance with student support or dissatisfaction with the PIRG. Thus individual students can reevaluate the program each registration period.

OSPIRG was weakened by a serious initial error. Because the student board was not able to find a person they believed qualified to serve as director, they hired two young staff attorneys and appointed one as interim director. This arrangement proved unsatisfactory. More than a law degree is needed to qualify as a PIRG director. Both resigned shortly after a permanent director was hired in December.

MPIRG had a different problem. They hired two coequal staff directors, both extremely qualified, and appointed one to direct research and one to be in charge of legal matters. Unfortunately, a dual directorate seemed to increase the administrative burden and decrease the efficiency and decisiveness of the organization. Late in the spring of 1972 the MPIRG student board appointed a coordinator to handle all administrative matters and to take over tactical planning. The legal and research directors retained responsibility for their respective areas.

The difficulties encountered by the first PIRGs were not unexpected. MPIRG and OSPIRG were pioneers and, as such, had to find their way. But the important fact to focus on is that both overcame their most serious weaknesses and grew stronger as the school year progressed. As students and staff began to realize the potential of the PIRG, minor problems faded and the organization began to blend into an effective team. In addition, the problems they encountered and their solutions to them provide a valuable guide to new PIRGs.

Despite the confusion involving internal organization, OSPIRG and MPIRG scored several significant victories during their first year. More significantly, they are engaged in a number of long-term summer study projects which will lay the foundation for sweeping actions during the 1972–73 school year. The following list describes a few of the projects already completed and the most important studies presently under way.

MPIRG Projects

LEGAL ACTIONS

1. MPIRG sued to force the Republican and Democratic Farmer-Labor parties to publish the dates and times and locations of precinct caucuses in daily newspapers throughout the state and to broadcast the same information over all radio and television stations. The suit was brought under a state law requiring publication of this information two weeks in advance of the caucuses. MPIRG alleged that in some counties no publication had occurred. Although the suit was denied, the court urged both parties to disseminate more information about the caucuses. Resulting newspaper and television reports about the suit also helped publicize the caucuses.

2. MPIRG sued to permit a nineteen-year-old to run for electoral office. The Minnesota constitution at present bars anyone under twenty-one from holding office even though eighteen-year-olds can vote. MPIRG's claim was denied, and it eventually appealed all the way to the United States Supreme Court, which upheld the lower court order. MPIRG is now preparing legislation to declare eighteen as the age of majority.

ACTION PROJECTS AND RESEARCH REPORTS

1. MPIRG prepared a manual for use by conservationists in state hearings on the setting of ambient air standards for Minnesota. These hearings were required by the federal clean air bill and the standards adopted had to conform to minimum federal requirements. The manual was used by citizen groups all over the state and became the basis for much of the testimony presented at the implementation hearings.

65

2. In cooperation with student groups, including several Girl Scout troops, MPIRG has conducted food pricing comparisons on stores throughout the state. (See Chapter 9 for details on retail price comparisons.)

3. MPIRG conducted a toy safety survey whose thoroughness attracted national attention. Toys in major department stores were examined for hazards and the names of stores carrying defective toys were widely disseminated. This report was one factor in the Food and Drug Administration's decision to appoint a citizen board to monitor the sale of unsafe toys. Even though these citizen boards have little power, they are a step in the right direction.

4. MPIRG staff members and student volunteers are investigating employment agencies that discriminate on grounds of sex. When sufficient evidence is collected, they intend to file suit under Title VII of the 1964 Civil Rights Act.

5. A major review of occupational health and safety laws and enforcement practices in Minnesota is being conducted by MPIRG in cooperation with individual unions and the state AFL-CIO.

6. Numerous other MPIRG projects are under way, including studies of pesticide usage, land use, natural resource management, the Hennepin County jail system, and available health-care facilities in the Twin Cities area.

OSPIRG Projects

1. In the course of a two-month study of Portland auto repair practices, an OSPIRG research team uncovered enough evidence of fraud and deception to warrant a full-scale investigation by the local district attorney's office and subsequent action against the principal offenders. Using cars certified by automotive education departments at several local colleges, the OSPIRG team found that over 60 percent of the shops visited were padding their esti-

mates with needless and nonexistent replacements and repairs. As a result of this study, documented in a ten-page OSPIRG brief, several major shops signed Assurances of Voluntary Compliance with the DA's Consumer Protection Division.*

2. OSPIRG staff and students, in collaboration with a University of Oregon professor, produced a report on state meat inspection practices which documented numerous shortcomings, recommended a series of major reforms, and received widespread press coverage throughout the state. The Department of Agriculture called the report "fair and accurate" and has since exercised its option and turned over all responsibility for state meat inspection to the federal government.

3. An OSPIRG-sponsored investigation of automobile dealers' advertising and sales practices caught several major dealers using deceptive "bait and switch" techniques or otherwise intentionally misrepresenting their products to the consumer. The study was accorded considerable attention by the media and resulted in compliance agreements between several dealers and the DA's office.

---

* See Appendix 6.

5 HOW TO ORGANIZE

The techniques used to build support for a Public Interest Research Group depend on size, diversity, and type of school. Normally, small, homogeneous colleges are easier to organize than large universities. Boarding schools are easier than commuting campuses and four-year colleges generally provide stronger support bases than junior colleges, again largely because of continuity. Advice and assistance on organizing a PIRG is available from the Washington, D.C., PIRG (see Appendix 1 for address).

An organizing effort usually begins with a small group of interested students on each campus willing to spend long hours planning, discussing, and proselytizing. Of course, the organizing experience is not all hard work. Meeting students from other schools with different backgrounds is a valuable learning experience, as is the knowledge gained in helping put together a statewide movement. The most important quality needed is dedication.

In Minnesota a group of fifteen students worked five months before gaining widespread support. In West Virginia, the organizing effort spanned more than the school year, lasting sixteen months altogether. At the same time as organizers are working on their own campuses, they should be contacting students at other schools within their state. To coordinate strategies, representatives from each school should meet periodically with their counterparts.

In most cases, it is important that organizing efforts be conducted at all the schools in the region, or at least a majority of them, not just on a single campus. Simultaneous petition drives create a multiplier effect as students at one school learn of the PIRG effort at other schools. This strategy also eliminates the risk of failing at the lead school and setting a bad precedent for other area schools. In addition, the PIRG idea will seem less strange and more plausible to administrators if other schools are also in the process of adopting it.

States with small student populations can organize more rapidly than larger states and they need fewer organizers. VPIRG (Vermont) passed from preliminary organizing to final approval in the space of six weeks. The three largest schools in Montana were organized by about twenty-five students in a period of three months. By contrast, PIRGIM (Michigan), with about five hundred student organizers on its three campuses, spent most of a year organizing. Vermont has a student population of 14,500; Montana 25,000; Michigan over 300,000. What is more, the largest school in Michigan has three times as many students as the whole state of Vermont and almost double Montana's student population. Although school size is an important factor in determining the pace of a PIRG campaign, timing is also affected by geography, the level of student activism, and administration openness. There are no set schedules to determine a campus's readiness for a PIRG campaign. But one fact is certain: until large numbers of students accept the PIRG idea, it will not be possible to obtain widespread support.

When beginning an organizing effort, the strength or weakness of the core group is decisive. It should include students from all segments of the campus, especially the newspaper and student

MODEL TIMETABLE*

1st Week   Introduction of the student PIRG plan to students on various campuses throughout the state or region. At the end of the first week, state or regional meeting to bring schools together to discuss the need for a PIRG, the necessity for unity, and the strategy for the statewide or regional effort.

2nd Week   Explanation of the PIRG plan to students on all campuses by news articles and other media. Development of core groups on each campus not contacted during the first week.

3rd Week   Second state or regional meeting. Initial phase of outlining specific PIRG model and proposal. Drafting of petition and design of new publicity.

4th and 5th Weeks   More intense effort to notify students of the effort under way. Low-key publicity campaign, intensifying and climaxing with accent on the upcoming petition campaign. Third state or regional meeting.

6th Week   Petition drive.

7th and 8th Weeks   Completion of petition drive with greater than 50 percent support in each school. Fourth state or regional meeting. Development of strategy to be used in approaching governing boards.

9th Week   Beginning of negotiations for administration approval; the length of time negotiations last depends on who has to be negotiated with.

legislature. While it may be self-gratifying for a small group of students to think they can form a PIRG, it is also a risky and self-defeating illusion. At each campus where this conceit has been practiced, the PIRG drive has failed. Unless the student community is kept informed of the organizing effort, the PIRG proposal

---

*The timetable is, of course, only a model. The actual time will be determined by the circumstances peculiar to each effort.

probably won't be accepted. But if students are aware of its existence and informed gradually of its potential, support during the petition drive and before the administration usually will be forthcoming.

Various campus groups initially may feel threatened by "another new group" seeking student support. Unwarranted animosity can be avoided by opening the avenues for cooperation at the outset and making clear the aims and objectives of the Public Interest Research Group. If the plan is presented correctly, student governments, women's groups, and minority groups will support the organizing effort. Each has an interest in creating a strong action-oriented organization to pursue public interest causes.

In order to bring PIRG to campus, the organizing group first must obtain a convincing show of student support. This can be accomplished by a referendum or petition drive. Preceding either of these should be several weeks of publicity and education efforts. Every such campaign requires money to pay for leaflets, posters, and office expenses. Therefore the first task is to raise money.

Fund Raising

PIRG organizing drives come in all varieties, from shoestring operations to elaborate productions costing several thousand dollars. The first two PIRG campaigns, in Oregon and Minnesota, had expenses in excess of $5,000, the largest portion of which was phone bills. By contrast, the VPIRG effort cost less than $1,000. Similar campaigns in New Jersey, West Virginia, and South Carolina were managed for under $2,000. During the same period, Texas, Washington, and Massachusetts PIRG campaigns cost in the neighborhood of $5,000 each. The cost of a particular PIRG drive is determined by two factors: the size of the organizing effort (that is, the number of students and schools involved in the plan) and the resources of the PIRG organizers.

Some of the money to fund a PIRG drive can be obtained

from participating student governments, student unions, and ecology and consumer clubs. Normally, these contributions will not be sufficient to fund the entire effort. Additional money can be raised from interested faculty members, off-campus donors, and committed student organizers. Also, the sale of bumper stickers, books, buttons, and silk-screen posters can help raise funds. A word of caution: while a serious organizing effort cannot operate without funds, PIRG organizers should resist the temptation to mount a slick, flashy campaign. For both practical and philosophical reasons, Madison Avenue salesmanship and big-budget spending are totally antithetical to the spirit of public interest work.

The expenses of the campaign, of course, can be minimized by obtaining donations of skills, facilities, and materials. PIRG organizers should try to obtain free office space, a mimeograph machine, use of a school telephone, and access to low-cost printing supplies. Often there is free space available in off-campus religious facilities, like Newman Centers and Wesley Houses. These same centers can provide additional facilities useful to a nascent PIRG. In many states, student PIRGs have received donations of time and materials from carpenters, advertising people, lawyers, photographers, and other concerned citizens.

Publicity

Students will not give away money to a cause unless they understand and believe in it. The PIRG organizers must convey through their publicity campaign a sophisticated prescription for student action and motivate students to participate in the plan. Where opposition develops the publicity effort must counter arguments against the PIRG concept.

There are usually dozens of campus and community groups competing for student support. It is critical that the PIRG organizing effort stand out and avoid falling into the category of "just another group." The publicity campaign must convince students that Public Interest Research Groups signal an entirely new direction in the student movement and are worthy of support. It is important that the publicity campaign does not encourage students to sign petitions impulsively, but rather that it makes students aware of the values and benefits of the PIRG plan.

From the outset, the group must determine the best means to achieve maximum impact. Since the organizing effort may last for several months, the tempo of the publicity campaign must be carefully established. New posters and leaflets which can maintain the pace of the effort and hold attention should be prepared and displayed. A consistent theme in the posters and leaflets throughout the campaign may be helpful in establishing an identity for the PIRG organizing effort. In Oregon and Minnesota the slogans "Environmental Preservation," "Consumer Protection," and "Corporate Responsibility" were repeated again and again. The posters, buttons, and leaflets used in Minnesota were printed in combinations of green, black, and orange. The students soon identified these colors with the Minnesota PIRG. A graphic symbol appearing on material may also serve a similar purpose.*

WVSPIRG (West Virginia) and Western Penn PIRG (Pittsburgh) printed four-page newspapers complete with photographs which they distributed by the thousand during the petition drive. WashPIRG (Washington) took full-page newspaper advertisements in the school newspaper at the University of Washington. One of the most effective of these was a series of photographs of poverty and pollution with stanzas from "America the Beautiful" accompanying each picture. TexPIRG (Texas) created "PIRG-MAN," a fighter for social justice, whose cartoon exploits dramatized the PIRG's future exploits. Whatever the medium, emphasis should be placed on hard, factual information rather than clichés.

---

* See Appendix 5 for examples of PIRG organizing materials.

HOW TO ORGANIZE

Discussion groups in dormitories, sororities, and fraternities, as well as in student unions, give students an opportunity to find out the details of the plan and how they can become involved. In addition, any questions or objections they may have can be aired and resolved during these sessions.

The campus newspaper and radio and television stations are invaluable sources of effective publicity. Very early in the effort, students should meet with representatives of each medium and explain the PIRG. Local newspapers and television and radio stations should be contacted, especially in commuter schools where students are linked more closely to the community. Plan to send out press releases on a regular basis and make every effort to gain editorial support. Besides the additional publicity the press can generate during the petitioning period, it is essential to contact newsmen because the eventual success of the PIRG will depend in large part on its ability to inform the public of the PIRG's actions and to influence public opinion.

Together with these traditional methods of publicity, more novel efforts are helpful in attracting student support. For example, at the University of Minnesota, students set up an elaborate multimedia presentation in the courtyard of the architecture building. An eight-minute filmstrip highlighted the effort. Giant green-and-orange banners silk-screened with the phrases "Environmental Quality," "Consumer Protection," and "Corporate Responsibility" were hung. Photographs, mobiles, and posters completed the display.

At Southern Illinois University, Buckminster Fuller's home campus, students constructed domes to advertise the Southern Illinois Public Interest Research Group.

At Oregon State University, students built a visual display depicting the effect of industrial sewage in a nearby river. The display was augmented by an explanation of how OSPIRG could solve the sewage problem by monitoring the industrial effluent and pressing for conformity to state and federal water quality regulations.

Pittsburgh students obtained publicity both at school and in the community by presenting a series of guest lecturers from state and local government agencies who conducted seminars on problems susceptible to solution by citizen action. In Boston, MassPIRG East used prerecorded spot announcements on a local FM station which had a large student audience. WMPIRG (Western Massachusetts) students filmed their own television show, which they showed on closed-circuit television in the student union.

The possibilities for such projects are limitless. The success or failure of the publicity campaign, however, should be measured less by its aesthetic impact than by its ability to provide students with a solid grasp of the goals and aims of the PIRG.

The Petition Drive

A petition drive to raise student fees will not be an easy task. Its success hinges on the efficacy of the publicity campaign and the ability of the petitioners to gain support on a one-to-one basis. The petitioners must strike a balance between oversell, which becomes obnoxious and counterproductive, and undersell, which becomes timid and ineffective. The petitioners must understand fully the concept of a Public Interest Research Group and be able to make clear the details of the plan.*

The complete understanding of the petitioners cannot be left to chance. In PIRG campaigns, petitioner booklets were prepared describing the rationale, structure, and goals of the group. The booklets were designed to give petitioners a working knowledge of the PIRG plan, plus additional hints on how to secure support.

* See Appendix 4 for hints on petitioning techniques.

HOW TO ORGANIZE

Lists of the most typical questions to be expected and their answers were included along with other information. Petitioners were asked to study the booklet and then attend a session at which members of the organizing committee answered questions and simulated petitioning situations.

Organization of the Petition Drive

The petition drive must be a well-coordinated effort in order to make the most efficient use of each petitioner's time. Before petitioning begins, establish when and where large groups of students can be found. In Texas, New Jersey, Iowa, eastern Massachusetts, and Minnesota, campuses were divided into three areas: university living areas, traffic centers, and classrooms.

UNIVERSITY LIVING AREAS

Dormitories, fraternities, sororities, and off-campus apartments are useful places to obtain support because they provide opportunities for individual and group contact. Make every effort to establish a liaison in each living group as early as possible. Frequently there are organized residence hall councils which can act as a source for these initial contacts.

It is advisable for students to petition within their own living groups, where they already have personal contacts. Students who live in dormitories frequently have a different perspective than students who live in Greek houses or off-campus. At Oregon State University, some dormitories had as many as three PIRG representatives on each floor. As a result, several dormitories registered 100 percent support. The same pattern has repeated itself at school after school during the 1971–72 organizing campaign.

TRAFFIC CENTERS

In large, predominantly commuter universities, petitioning in living units will not be enough. In order to contact students,

77

identify the points on campus where many students congregate or pass through on their way to classes. These areas are the student traffic centers: student unions, libraries, heavily used walkways between buildings; in commuter campuses, student traffic centers also include bus stops, train stations, and parking areas.

In Pittsburgh (Western Penn PIRG), Massachusetts (WMPIRG), and Vermont (VPIRG), organizers supplied each traffic center with either a table or a portable petition stand. A banner, visual display, or poster was set up to attract attention, and literature explaining the PIRG plan was made easily accessible. Be sure to take into consideration the times of day and the days of the week that students pass through these centers.

Students at Oregon State University and the University of Minnesota used on-the-spot reports and computer analyses to help determine the effectiveness of all centers. Every evening the petition information was tallied and a computer analysis run to gauge the results of each center.

CLASSROOMS

At the University of Minnesota, where more than 90 percent of the students are commuters, it was found that classroom buildings were heavily inhabited from 9:00 A.M. to 3:00 P.M. The libraries were used most often in the evening between 6:00 P.M. and 10:00 P.M. At the two largest universities in Oregon, many students live within walking distance of the campus. Though they were reluctant to sign petitions in the morning on their way to class, petitioners found students willing to sign on their way home, when they were less pressed for time.

Some traffic centers lose their effectiveness after a time because they are frequented by the same students. When petitioning success falls off in an area, the effort should be transferred to a new location. Failure to move can result in discouragement for petitioners and a crucial loss of potential signatures.

HOW TO ORGANIZE

In both Oregon and Minnesota, petitioners were organized into teams responsible for a single traffic center. When the petition effort was moved, the group moved as a unit. This arrangement simplified scheduling and allowed the group to mold itself into a cohesive team. Petitioning was most effective when several students manned the petition center at once, and when they worked for two-hour periods.

For a thorough organizing effort, petition large lecture sections and seminar classes. Sympathetic professors may allow a student speaker five or ten minutes at the beginning of a class to explain the PIRG concept and enlist support. After a short explanation, pass out individual petition forms with space for only one signature. Individual petition forms allow petitioners to reach every student and minimize the use of class time. They also eliminate the confusion of trying to gather signatures as students rush in and out of class. Individual forms can also be used effectively to petition large audiences in auditoriums or at sporting events.

Petition Forms

The petition form is an important part of the overall campaign. It should be clear and concise. The following suggestions may be helpful.

1. Include a well-defined statement of purpose and a short explanation of the financial mechanism.
2. Provide a space for student names, addresses, and identification numbers so that signatures can be verified.
3. Number each petition form individually to facilitate record keeping and minimize the possibility of loss.
4. Record the petitioner's name and the numbers of the petitions he takes each time a new petition leaves the office.
5. Make each petitioner responsible for every petition checked out in his/her name. Do not leave petition forms

unattended on tables or tacked up on walls. If a petition is lost, all of the signatures are lost with it.

Petition No.———

MODEL PETITION AND RESOLUTION

We, the undersigned, stand resolved that the ———— Public Interest Research Group (———— PIRG) be established:

—The purpose of ———— PIRG shall be to articulate and pursue through the media, the institutions of government, the courts, and other legal means the concerns of students on issues of general public interest.

—Issues will include environmental preservation, human rights, consumer protection, and the role of corporation and government agencies in the lives of the average citizen.

— ———— PIRG shall be nonpartisan, nonprofit, and student controlled.

—It shall be financed by an increase in student fees of one dollar per student per quarter (or two dollars per semester).

—Any student who does not wish to participate shall be entitled to a full refund during the third week of each quarter from an established public office of each campus.

We, students registered at the University of ————, hereby petition the Board of ———— of the University of ———— to authorize the formation of ———— PIRG.

NAME	ADDRESS	STUDENT NO.
1.		
2.		
3.		
4.		
5.		
6.		
7.		

HOW TO ORGANIZE

Post-petitioning Letdown

During the petition drive, interest on campus reaches its peak. The campus newspaper headlines petition totals, local radio and television stations feature the organizing effort, and hundreds of students join the effort. The original core group expands rapidly. At the University of Minnesota, for example, Minneapolis/St. Paul media zeroed in on the campus during the two-week petition period while the organizing group multiplied from fifteen to four hundred.

When the drive is completed and final tallies of the signatures are in, workers drift off to other activities, and the core group shrinks back to a few dozen of the most committed students. The intensity of the petition effort, coupled with accumulated class work, is a prime reason for the falloff.

The core group, of course, then turns its efforts to gain approval from the university and its governing board. As the proposal winds its way through various committees toward final approval, student spokesmen are required to attend dozens of meetings. If legislative approval is needed, a major lobbying effort may have to be undertaken. But this work is specialized and, for the most part, demands more commitment than the average student is prepared to make. Student research and action projects can be developed to maintain interest in the PIRG. Student researchers can gather data on environmental or consumer problems to provide a foundation for the work of the professional staff. Additionally, students can identify the agencies responsible for dealing with these problems.

With the help of interested faculty members, classes can be established to teach students the workings of the governmental system, the legal system in America, how a corporation operates, and how specific problems can be solved. Additional projects are outlined in Chapter 9.

6 GETTING UNDER WAY

Administrative Approval

After a successful petition campaign, student organizers should make plans to secure approval from the appropriate administrative authority. The first step is to identify who has the power to approve a fee increase and what procedures must be followed to obtain approval. The administrative structure for higher education is different in every state, but, in general, private schools are governed by individual boards of trustees while state-supported institutions are controlled by regents or boards of higher education.

Sometimes the power to increase fees in public schools is left to the state legislature, and to obtain a fee increase new legislation is needed. A different situation occurs when the board of regents has the power to raise fees but refuses to exercise it without an indication of legislative support. In either case, individual legislators should be persuaded to indicate support for the program by meetings with the PIRG student organizers who come from their own districts. The impact of the youth vote, especially at the party caucus level, should guarantee a warm reception from most legislators. To show support for the plan, where power to raise fees lies with the regents, individual legislators can phone, write, or wire the regents or act as a body and pass a resolution commending PIRG. Appendix 7 contains a copy of the resolution unanimously passed by the New Jersey Assembly.

In many schools the student senate or some other student group has the power to raise fees. In these situations PIRG organizers should bypass the administration and seek student approval directly. Michigan State, Syracuse University, and Boston College passed the PIRG proposal by student vote alone. Where students obtain greater control over activity fee systems, this method of obtaining support should become more common.

It has been found that even overwhelming support expressed by the petition campaign does not guarantee approval from an administrative board. The board will examine closely each aspect of the proposal. One should anticipate a myriad of questions from board members and prepare answers to them before formally seeking approval. An indication of support for the PIRG proposal from government officials, community groups, and faculty members can also help persuade the board about the merits of the plan. It is important, however, that this support be bipartisan to avoid implications of political alliance.

Because boards of education are usually attuned to the opinions of citizen groups, it is also important to seek community support. Too often in the past, students have unnecessarily alienated sectors of society, not because of what they said, but because of the way they said it. If the community feels a sense of identity with the PIRG, if it realizes that the PIRG's interests are its own, many traditional barriers can be broken down, and rapport can be established between students and community. Once the PIRG is approved, if it is to be successful, it has to influence public opinion, and all avenues of communication are essential.

If past experience is a true guide, one of the most important concerns of the administration will be the educational value of the

PIRG. While it may seem obvious that all the activities of a PIRG have some educational value, and that many of the activities may be extraordinarily valuable, a strong faculty endorsement goes a long way toward assuring administrative approval.

There are many ways to gain faculty support:

1. A general mailing explaining the merits of a PIRG to all faculty members.

2. Personal interviews with faculty members.

3. Presentations to various faculty forums, such as the faculty senate, administrative councils, departmental meetings, etc.

It is important for supportive faculty members to let board members know what they think. They may want to write to the board as individuals or collectively as departments to register their support. A faculty petition may also be filed with the board when the students are presenting their case. If the board believes that the faculty will be involved with the PIRG, they may be more assured of its educational purposes.

After obtaining student support, PIRG organizers usually spend several weeks developing and refining the PIRG proposal before they seek formal administrative approval. The final proposal should be printed and distributed to each administrator whose support is needed. This proposal should include

1. A well-defined statement of purpose.

2. A detailed outline of the PIRG's organizational structure.

3. A statement of the educational value of the PIRG.

4. A legal brief examining the tax question.

5. Copies of endorsements from prominent community, state, or national figures.

6. The proposed budget for the PIRG.*

For many administrative boards, the educational value of the

---

* Information and copies of proposals, while they last, are available from state PIRGs. See Appendix 1 for addresses.

PIRG will be the decisive factor. Others will take the educational value for granted and focus on tax questions. (See Chapter 7 for an extended discussion of both these important questions.)

MODEL STATEMENT OF PURPOSE AND OBJECTIVES

__PIRG will undertake to identify and evaluate issues involving public policy decisions, including social planning, institutional regulation and control, and matters of individual rights which affect substantial numbers of people. __PIRG will determine the alternative solutions available, in order to determine what course of action __PIRG should take to bring about corporate, governmental, and other institutional changes that are necessary to further the public interest.

Action taken by __PIRG will consist of a coordinated effort of analysis and research; public education; active representation before legislative bodies and before administrative and regulatory agencies; and litigation—where such actions are warranted—to achieve the goals of this group. It will not become involved in internal campus disputes or disputes between campuses.

The general areas of __PIRG concern will include consumer protection, resource planning, occupational safety, protection of natural areas and environmental quality, racial and sexual discrimination, landlord/tenant relations, delivery of health care, freedom of information in government, and similar matters of urgent or long-range concern to the welfare of the people of the State of _____.

Besides educational or tax considerations, boards may inquire into aspects of the plan ranging from the propriety of using student fees to the validity of the signatures on the petitions. Some possible questions raised by board members may include the following:

1. Is the PIRG plan unfair, since it forces those students who do not wish to support the PIRG to go to the trouble of obtaining refunds?

There are several strong reasons to support the contention

that the PIRG proposal is not only fair, but that it is a definite improvement over most student fee plans.

First, unlike most other student fees which are instituted by university fiat, the PIRG fee is initiated by students on the basis of student support expressed in a referendum or petition drive. If a majority of students do not support the plan, it should not be adopted. However, no matter how many students support the PIRG proposal, inevitably some will object to it and often their opposition will focus on the funding mechanism. The question that must be answered, therefore, is whether the majority of students have the right to force all students to pay and to require the dissenting minority to go to the trouble of obtaining a refund. Or, to phrase the question more philosophically, can a majority ever legitimately require a minority to act against its wishes?

Clearly the answer to the second question must be yes, with the caveat that the majority cannot legitimately infringe on the basic rights of the minority. In a democracy the majority has the prerogative to determine procedures so long as minority rights are respected. The rights of dissenters are protected by their right to obtain refunds from a well-publicized, easily accessible office on campus. Even if a few students are inconvenienced, in a choice between inconveniencing the minority slightly and massively inconveniencing the majority by forcing them to hold a new fundraising campaign each term, majority rights must prevail. Therefore, the answer to the question of whether the majority of students can require the minority to ask for a refund is yes, provided the refunds are easily obtained.

A second line of reasoning leads to the same conclusion. If majority rights are to count for anything, they should grant the majority the right to have about three weeks to persuade the minority and freshmen of the worth of the PIRG plan. The three weeks between registration and the refund period gives the majority this opportunity. Without it, the majority and minority are placed on exactly equal footing with absolutely no weight granted to students who voted or petitioned to implement the PIRG proposal.

There is a third reason why the orderly funding mechanism of the PIRG plan should be adopted. Without a standardized collection procedure, the educational value of the plan will be diluted. It is not the purpose of a PIRG to train students in the art of fund raising. If students have to mount a full-scale publicity drive and fund-raising campaign each quarter or semester to keep the PIRG afloat, they will have little time for research, study, and investigation.

Moreover, as a practical matter, it is impossible to carry out a successful fund-raising drive each registration period. Just like a football team which has winning and losing seasons, at some point student fund raisers would be bound to be weak or inept in the arts of publicity and persuasion. At this point the PIRG would collapse. Imagine an athletic team being run on this basis. A few losing seasons and the team would be out of business. Even with a winning record, a team might have trouble collecting money during the off-season. Also, repeated fund-raising efforts utilize valuable time and energies which could be better spent working on substantive issues.

Fourth, while professionals are willing to accept low salaries to do work they believe in, they need some measure of financial security. Even though all students who do not choose to pay can get refunds, the PIRG funding mechanism offers more security than tin cup collections by amateur fund raisers. Experience in Oregon, Minnesota, Vermont, and Missouri shows that professionals will risk their careers to work for student PIRGs that have secure funding provisions.

In summary, it is clear that there are strong, persuasive arguments in favor of the PIRG fee mechanism. The objection of unfairness raised against it loses its validity if the opportunity to obtain a refund is fairly offered. However, additional safeguards can be adopted that offer students and universities additional protection. One such provision might provide for the severance of the contract between the university and the PIRG if a majority of students demanded refunds.

2. Will raising student fees for a Public Interest Research Group open the door for other student groups?

Because other groups may want to use the same petition process to raise fees to establish their own organizations, the board may fear that it will be deluged by similar requests. If other groups can gain overwhelming support from students, faculty, and many facets of the community, plus exhibit clearly the educational value in their programs, the board may well agree to raise student fees for those purposes, too. But the process itself eliminates all but the most determined groups. Therefore, it is doubtful that an unmanageable number of requests will come before the board. Those that do may be examined under the same standards applied to the PIRG.

3. Will the PIRG's refund provision force the university to offer refunds on other mandatory fees?

The answer is clearly no. Each fee request stands or falls on its own merits. There is no universal principle involved. A board can permit one fee to operate on the checkoff basis, another to be mandatory, and a third to offer refunds. Nevertheless, boards may worry about setting a precedent for refunding any fees at all.

This problem can be solved by placing the responsibility for refunding money with the PIRG and *not* with the university. The PIRG has a binding responsibility to offer a refund because this is the funding mechanism students approved. As far as the board is concerned, the fee increase is mandatory. However, if the PIRG offers the refund itself, the board does not set a binding precedent for refunding other mandatory fees, and if the PIRG doesn't refund, the contract is broken.

4. Should a university collect fees for an organization it does not control?

Most universities already do. The obvious example at most schools is the collection of fees for health insurance or food contracts. However, there is a better answer to this question. Since students control the PIRG it cannot be said to be outside university control, even though it is outside *administration* control.

Moreover, at most schools administrators would not attempt to claim that they directly control all student activities. It is only at a few reactionary institutions that the school newspaper, the student union, and the student government are under administration control. It is true that if one of these organizations violates the law, the university can enact sanctions against it. But the same is true with the PIRG. The administration can always terminate the contract with the PIRG to collect fees if it has just cause. Therefore, ultimate control over the university-PIRG relationship remains with the administration or board of trustees.

5. How does the board know that the petition signatures are valid?

Attesting to the validity of petition signatures can be done in several ways. In Oregon, students had a statistician take a random sample of two hundred signatures from each university to determine what percentage of the two hundred were fully registered students. Less than half of 1 percent were not fully enrolled. This percentage was applied to the total number of petition signatures in order to estimate the number of valid signatures. Another method of verification is to use a computer. Each signature is keypunched into a computer which cross-references each name with the list of duly enrolled students. The computer process is by far the most accurate, but the expense and time of punching out each name are significant. Organizers should weigh the benefits of each method carefully.

In most states where the PIRG plan has been approved, administrative boards did not question the validity of individual signatures. They were content with the fact that an overwhelming number of students had expressed support for the proposal, and whether the total was 51 or 65 percent of the student body did not seem important. Nevertheless, the larger the margin of support, the stronger the case for approval, if any opposition is encountered.

6. How will the board know whether the students are supporting the PIRG a year from now?

Most PIRGs provide in their articles of incorporation that any campus where 50 percent of the students requested refunds would no longer participate. This provision is an effective internal check on the PIRG as well as a good indicator of student response.

7. How can students be involved in the plan besides paying the fee increase?

Obviously, not every student has the opportunity or the inclination to become involved actively in a PIRG project. There is no way that the professional staff, even with the help of interested faculty, can supervise the activities of more than a few hundred students at any one time. Therefore, the professional staff must seek out aggressive student leaders and train them to lead other students, if it is to achieve a multiplier effect and involve large masses of students.

Students who do work on projects may perform basic research and data-collection functions, or assist with legal brief-writing, or appear before state or municipal regulatory agencies. Additionally, the most interested students can run for election on local boards of directors or serve as volunteers working on local board committees. Students who are too busy to become actively involved, but who have areas of concern, can suggest projects to their local boards.

There are no certain formulas that guarantee administration

approval. But if the details for the plan have been thoroughly worked out and if strong student support has been received, most administrators will find it difficult to deny students the right to use their own money to work constructively to effect social betterment. It is especially difficult for administrators who have condemned student demonstrations in the past to turn around and deny a request to permit lawful, educational research by concerned students. However, some boards of trustees or regents may ignore student sentiment and oppose the PIRG plan. If this situation should occur, PIRG organizers should study the board's stated reasons carefully. They may provide a basis for a law suit to eliminate all required university fees and to place all activities on a purely voluntary basis. Where all fees are voluntary, a voluntarily funded PIRG would not be placed at a disadvantage. There is no doubt that in such a case the PIRG would receive more support than most other university activities.

Election of the Local Board

Each school participating in the PIRG plan should conduct an election to select representatives to the local board. These elections may be held before or after administration approval is obtained. However, to conserve money, the election probably should not be held until after final approval is obtained. Elections may be held independently of regular campus elections, but it is easier to generate a large turnout if the election is held at the same time as regular student elections rather than if a special referendum for the PIRG board is held separately.

It is important that elections do not open splits among conflicting campus factions. At all times the focus of the PIRG must be external, directed away from internal campus issues and personalities, toward public issues. A sure way to bring about an early collapse is to permit old campus rivalries to infiltrate and divide the PIRG on issues which are not its concern.

GETTING UNDER WAY

Schools should schedule their elections on a rotating basis so that at no one time are more than half the schools holding elections. This insures that at least half the members of the state board are experienced. A complete turnover each election period would destroy the stability of the state board.

Recruiting and Hiring the Professional Staff

As soon as final approval is certain, the state board should begin to hire the full-time staff. Thousands of presently employed professionals and new graduates from college and from graduate and professional schools are searching for work in the public interest arena. There are several ways to recruit these people to fill job openings in the PIRG. The best way to contact graduating seniors is a letter, with an accompanying descriptive flyer, to university placement officers. The best times to recruit graduates are the late fall and winter. By spring most students have already located jobs. Because many PIRGs are not ready to hire until spring and because the expenses of a mailing to all placement officers is high, the national PIRG has established a job clearinghouse (see Appendix 1 for address). While the national PIRG will collect résumés and send them to the state PIRGs, under no circumstances will it hire or participate directly in the hiring of staff for a state PIRG.

All hiring should be done by members of the state board. When necessary, faculty and community advisers can be called in to provide support. The director should be the first person hired; once hired, he or she should participate in all employment decisions. This is to insure that obvious personality conflicts are avoided and that staff members acknowledge the role of the director.

A strong director is an essential ingredient of a successful PIRG. Ideally a PIRG director should have all the following qualities: a strong sense of social justice; leadership and self-start-

93

ing ability; the courage to act on convictions; the political sensitivity to build community support; the youth (in mind or body or both) to relate well to students; the experience to command respect and to handle difficult administrative and personnel decisions; past public interest credentials; good professional and organizing abilities; tremendous stamina; good public speaking abilities with a flair for publicizing; and talent and speed as a writer. Obviously, few people can meet all these qualifications. But student board members should keep these criteria in mind and measure potential directors against them. Each PIRG will have to determine for itself which skill is paramount. For example, the larger the PIRG, the more important administrative ability becomes. The more hostile the surrounding community, the more crucial political sensitivity and public relations ability become.

Staff members probably will be younger and less experienced than the director. But they, too, should be chosen following the same criteria, with the difference that administrative abilities are less important. The kinds of professional skills needed will depend on what problems are identified as critical in each state. Since the remedies to most problems require action by courts, legislatures, or administrative agencies, lawyers are an important part of the group. Other skills are also important, especially in the early months of the PIRG, when flexibility is essential. Each employee should be able to perform several different tasks and not be limited to a single narrow specialty.

Salary and contract vary depending on the experience of the individual and the wage scale of the area in which the group is located. Washington, D.C., PIRG attorneys earn $5,000 per year. MPIRG pays its professionals on a scale ranging from $9,500 to $12,500 per year, with need being the principal factor. MPIRG's legal director took a 50 percent pay cut to accept his $12,500 per year position. MPIRG will forward a copy of its budget, on request, to other PIRG boards. VPIRG pays its director $7,000 and is offering attorneys $6,000. Most other PIRGs are planning to pay salaries more in line with Vermont's salary scale than Minnesota's.

A balance must be struck between subsistence wages, which discourage all but the wealthy or the most committed and encourage only one- or two-year stays, and high salaries on a par with government or private firm salaries. As a rough rule, PIRG salaries can be 25 to 50 percent below the local wage scale without a diminution in the quality of potential staff members. Those who apply to PIRG usually rank salary low on their list of job criteria. It isn't money but the chance to harmonize their jobs with their value systems that brings people to PIRG.

7 TAX AND EDUCATION

Tax and educational considerations are paramount because they are the first and the highest hurdles the PIRGs have to clear to gain administrative approval. No board will sanction a student organization that might jeopardize the university's tax-exempt status. Similarly, most boards of education are empowered to authorize only educational activities. Therefore, unless the educational value of the PIRG can be demonstrated, the plan falls outside the purview of board authority and cannot be approved.

*Tax Considerations**

A PIRG WILL BE A NONPROFIT, TAX-EXEMPT CORPORATION

A Public Interest Research Group must be organized and operated under the laws of the state in which it is located. The Secretary of State's office, usually located at the state capitol, can supply information about the formation and operation of a nonprofit corporation. Since a nonprofit corporation which complies

---

* The following explanation is not meant to be complete. Because of the complexity of these questions, it is essential to enlist the aid of a law professor or community lawyer who specializes in tax work.

with appropriate federal and state tax laws is eligible for "tax-ex-empt status," it will not be required to pay corporate income tax. Depending on its activities, a Public Interest Research Group can seek tax-exempt status under 26 United States Code 501 (c) 3 or under 26 United States Code 501 (c) 4:

> 501 (c) 3 status is granted to corporations organized and operated exclusively for "religious, charitable, scientific, testing for public safety, literacy or educational pur-poses . . ."
> 501 (c) 4 status is accorded to corporations "not organ-ized for profit but operated exclusively for the promo-tion of social welfare."

SIMILARITIES AND DIFFERENCES BETWEEN 501 (c) 3 AND 501 (c) 4 STATUS

Besides granting tax exemption to corporations which qualify for either 501 (c) 3 or 501 (c) 4 status, the law gives an additional benefit to 501 (c) 3 corporations. Donors to these corporations are permitted to deduct the amount of their gift from their taxable in-come, thus lowering their personal income tax and giving them added incentive to make a contribution. No such privilege is ac-corded 501 (c) 4 corporations. Because of the tax benefits it con-veys to both the corporation and its patrons, 501 (c) 3 status is harder to acquire.

IS 501 (c) 3 OR 501 (c) 4 STATUS PREFERABLE FOR A STUDENT PIRG?

The answer to this question depends on how the PIRG in-tends to function. A PIRG with 501 (c) 4 status can lobby freely, litigate in almost every area, and conduct citizen organizing drives, but it cannot receive foundation funding or provide tax benefits to wealthy community residents who may donate money.

TAX AND EDUCATION

A PIRG with a 501 (c) 3 status can carry on public education efforts, litigate in many areas, research any issue, and confer a tax benefit for all donations, but cannot devote any substantial part of its activities to lobbying or to organizing efforts which would result in lobbying.

Obviously, 501 (c) 3 status would not benefit a student-supported PIRG because the three or four dollars each student donates is too small to amount to a significant tax savings. Since student contributions normally provide adequate support, the other 501 (c) 3 asset—foundation support—is canceled out by the loss of such important areas of action as lobbying and organizing citizens to lobby.

Based on these considerations, 501 (c) 4 status is probably the best form of organization for a student-supported Public Interest Research Group.

The benefit of tax deductability is significant only when donations are large. Foundations normally do not make grants to corporations which do not have 501 (c) 3 status, and wealthy donors usually want the benefit of personal tax deduction when they make gifts, which only a 501 (c) 3 corporation gives them.

At the same time that the law grants benefits, it also imposes certain constraints. Neither 501 (c) 3 nor 501 (c) 4 corporations may intervene in any political campaign on behalf of a candidate for public office. A 501 (c) 4 corporation may lobby freely and support or oppose legislation, but 501 (c) 3 status severely restricts lobbying. A *public* 501 (c) 3 organization can devote only an "insubstantial" part of its activities to lobbying. A *private* 501 (c) 3 group cannot lobby at all. ("Public" 501 (c) 3 status is accorded a 501 (c) 3 group that receives more than one-third of its contributions from the general public. "Private" status is granted to corporations supported by a few major contributors.)

The amount of money spent on lobbying is not a sufficient criterion to determine its substantiality; instead, all resources and activities of the corporation must be examined in relation to IRS standards.

An additional possibility under consideration by students in Oregon and Minnesota involves setting up two separate corporations. One corporation would apply for 501 (c) 3 status and carry out research, public education, and litigation (as permitted by the applicable tax law), while the other would seek 501 (c) 4 status for lobbying and other types of litigation. The 501 (c) 3 corporation would be able to attract foundation support, while the 501 (c) 4 corporation could carry out lobbying efforts and other litigation. A student PIRG simply does not need such support. Foundation money should be left for public interest groups which cannot get money any other way.

LEGAL STATUS OF UNIVERSITIES IN RELATION TO PIRG

All universities and colleges are tax-exempt corporations supported in part by private donations from individuals and foundations. The tax-deductibility of their gifts is essential. Private schools are also tax-exempt 501 (c) 3 corporations, and state schools, while they may have 501 (c) 3 status, are normally tax-exempt because they are institutions of the state. So a major question in the minds of most college administrators, regents, and trustees is whether the tax-exempt status of the institution could be jeopardized by any activities of the PIRG. The answer for both private and state schools is a resounding no.

If the PIRG is a 501 (c) 3 corporation, the question should never arise, since the activities of a 501 (c) 3 corporation do not adversely affect the tax status of another 501 (c) 3 corporation or of a state instrumentality. If the PIRG should exceed the permissible bounds of activity for a 501 (c) 3 corporation and engage in "substantial" lobbying activities or incorporate with a 501 (c) 4 status, the question still does not apply to schools which are considered state institutions. Such institutions have no restrictions on

100

their lobbying activities. Private schools, however, cannot afford to risk their 501 (c) 3 status.

Private universities will endanger their status *only* if they engage in a "substantial" amount of lobbying activities. Certainly 15 percent of an institution's activities would be viewed as substantial, but 1 percent probably would not. In general, a 5-percent rule is applied as a rough test and, as the next paragraphs will show, it would be difficult if not impossible for a PIRG to make up more than 1 percent of university activity.

Two points must be made with respect to the activities of a PIRG. First, the university only acts as a collecting agent for the research group. The money collected belongs to the PIRG; the university, while it has possession, has no control over the money. The money itself, and the activities it supports, are those of PIRG, not the university. Therefore, the status of the PIRG should in no way affect the university's own tax status if the university is only a collecting agent for the PIRG.

Second, even if the money were considered to belong to the university and the PIRG devoted all of its resources to lobbying, its activities would still not constitute a "substantial" portion of the university's total activities. "Substantial" has been interpreted to mean 5 percent of an organization's activities. A contribution of three to four dollars per student per year adds up to less than one-tenth of 1 percent of the school's total revenues. When all the resources and activities of the university are considered, this figure is even smaller. Therefore, neither a 501 (c) 3 nor a 501 (c) 4 PIRG endangers a private university's tax-exempt status.

The Educational Value of a PIRG

RESEARCH

The PIRG's major projects are under the direction of the professional staff, in consultation with faculty and community resource persons. However, much of the actual study is done by students, either during the academic year or during vacation periods.

The main thrust of the PIRG's research is obtaining existing information in the area under investigation. This research includes gathering documents, searching through government files, interviewing public officials, conducting statistical surveys, collecting samples, and performing laboratory analysis. Its educational value is obvious.

Too often in colleges and in universities theoretical constructs are erected with no grounding in empirical research. In a real sense, the PIRG serves as a bridge between theory and practice. For example, students researching a utility rate regulating agency or examining the biological effect of a particular pollutant in an estuary environment are forced to perform the most exacting kind of research before arriving at a conclusion that can be presented publicly to the press, legislature, or an administrative agency. Even learning *how* to do such research is a major educational benefit.

Further, the PIRG concept is built on the idea of interdisciplinary study. When any problem is researched, every possible angle must be examined and all interrelationships discovered. A single lawyer or a single group of biology students cannot hope to be able to research all sides of a problem. Hence, students from a broad spectrum of backgrounds, as well as a diverse group of professionals, are a requisite for the PIRG's success. Many science-oriented students tend to ignore liberal arts studies because of their "lack of relevance." Concurrently, many liberal arts majors feel that science is a complicated morass of cells, instruments, and technical jargon without human values. Consequently, the communication patterns between students in divergent disciplines are frequently superficial at best, if not nonexistent. The PIRG involvement provides a new impetus for interdisciplinary study.

In the same vein, the PIRG offers students from different institutions an opportunity to work together on common problems. Also, students are able to draw on the expertise of faculty on other campuses where a particular discipline or research program is emphasized. This consideration has unlimited potential to open channels of communication between students and faculty, between academic institutions, and between educational disciplines.

PUBLIC EDUCATION

An important educational consideration is the involvement of members of the community with the functions of the PIRG. Too often in the past, the citizenry has remained isolated from the universities and, as a result, has received a false or misleading impression of higher education. And too often students have been isolated from the activities and concerns of the ordinary citizen. Working together on projects of common concern facilitates a better understanding and develops rapport between students and the general public.

Students also gain valuable experience in the use of the public media to educate other students, the university, and the general public. This is accomplished through the use of public forums and local television and radio programs and by publicizing projects in campus, local, and state newspapers.

ADVOCACY

The key to a PIRG is effective advocacy for the public interest in policy decisions made by executive, legislative, and judicial bodies. The advocacy function of the PIRG is carried out primarily by the professional staff in two basic areas: administrative and legislative bodies, and courts of law.

Some students, especially those in graduate and professional schools, are particularly suited to aid the staff in its advocacy functions. Students involved at this level of the PIRG activity are called upon to testify before legislative and administrative hearings, draft model legislation, prepare memoranda, and do research. These action programs provide students with a valuable operational knowledge of the existing channels for social change as well as empirical experience.

8 THE HIGH SCHOOL PIRG

Many high school students share the same social concerns as their older sisters and brothers in college, yet they have even less opportunity to express them. Rigid high school curriculums and government structures have tended to prevent the formation of large-scale student organizations seriously concerned with finding solutions to social problems. Instead, high school activists have been forced to turn away from their own schools and find work with college and community groups. All too often this means doing the stamp licking, envelope stuffing, phone answering, message running, and similar tasks which older people are only too happy to turn over to eager high school volunteers. Of course, this sort of work is important and needs to be done, but as a continuous diet it becomes tiresome and high school students are capable of doing much more. As a result, many high school students drop out after an initial fling of social activism and return to the routine of school.

Fortunately, there are indications that this pattern is changing. During the 1970 student strike to protest the Cambodian invasion, the New York City high school coalition was the best organized, most cohesive group in the city. The underground high school press in many cities publishes quality newspapers with citywide readerships. During the summer of 1970, five high school students spent the summer researching conditions in nursing homes. They presented their findings to the Subcommittee on Long-Term Care of the Special Committee on Aging, appeared on nationwide television, and published a book entitled *Old Age: The Last Segregation* (Grossman Publishers and Bantam Books, 1971). In several states high school students have broadened their focus and have responded and helped form organizations with lasting social impact. In Connecticut, high school students provided much of the impetus behind a statewide organizing and fund-raising effort during the spring of 1971 which resulted in the creation of the Connecticut Citizen Action Group (CCAG). Ohio high school students, during the same period, were instrumental in the creation of the Ohio Public Interest Action Group (OPIAG). (See Appendix 1 for addresses of CCAG and OPIAG.) Vermont high school students in the Burlington area teamed with university students in the fall and winter of 1971 to form the Vermont Public Interest Research Group (VPIRG). High school students in many other states may be ready to undertake similar organizing efforts if the opportunity is presented to them. However, it must be recognized at the outset that there are special problems associated with high school organizing. Even more than is the case with college students, high school students suffer from the twin handicaps of lack of continuity and expertise. Without continuity, it is difficult to mount sustained efforts of organizing research and investigation. Also, without some degree of expertise either the research will be inferior or, once it is complete, students won't know how to use it. Another problem is that the high school year is usually longer and more inflexible than the university year, which automatically limits the scope of summer and extracurricular projects. Most high school students are limited by heavy class schedules and course requirements. Most schools still allow few elective courses and are strict about classroom attendance. Many schools have poor laboratory equipment, limited libraries, and no access to computer facilities. Even schools with these facilities may severely limit their extracurricular use by students. These handicaps tend to be overwhelming for most high school students, and as a result most spend very little time working on social problems.

High school students bear one additional burden which greatly impedes the construction of strong student organizations, that of not being taken seriously. Teachers and administrators often view fifteen- , sixteen- , and seventeen-year-olds as mere children, "too young to understand what it's really all about" and certainly too young to do anything about it. Consequently, they accord them less freedom and less respect than is given to university students. This lack of respect pervades most teacher-student relationships and makes for vastly differing views of the problems that students should be concerned with and working on.

The dangerous myth that high school students are "just kids" has been allowed to stand unchallenged for such a long time that many students, teachers, and parents have come to believe it and act accordingly. If only teachers and parents were caught up in this adolescent stretchout, a student activist could easily organize his or her fellow students around this issue and mount a campaign to overcome it. But because many students themselves are believers, it is difficult to achieve organizational break-throughs.

A cursory analysis of the myth of adolescent helplessness reveals its transparent falsehood. In many societies and, formerly in the United States as well, fifteen- to seventeen-year-olds assumed fully responsible adult roles. They married, raised families, started careers, and performed all the duties of citizens. But prolonged adolescence is good business since the young are prolific and impressionistic consumers. Teen-agers today are bombarded with advertisements slanted towards them that promise cures of acne, halitosis, and that dreaded disease, body odor. They are urged to drink cola, buy luxury or frilly clothes, cars, and records, and to attend movies. Over and over the ceaseless message to consume, consume, consume is repeated, and beneath the words whispers the subliminal message that the problem of skin blemishes is more important than hunger in Appalachia or that a good breath mint will solve a problem more serious than air pollution. High school girls, especially, have to guard against the philosophy that good grooming or the right dress equals sex appeal, which in turn means sure success. "Forget about goals or careers," these ads imply, "look good and get that date." All this serves to create tremendous self-directed concern in superficial areas and diverts students from directing their energies outwardly towards more significant problems. Also, this attitude reinforces students' view of themselves as immature "children" with all the other implications which generally accompany such a view.

In fact, most high school students are fully capable of perceiving and understanding social problems. Many have the time, energy, and commitment to find solutions to these problems. The challenge to the high school activist and to dedicated teachers and administrators as well is to find ways to coordinate and unleash these strengths.

The best way to get people involved in a program is to give them something interesting to do. Creative students should not be hard pressed to discover avenues for action for themselves and ways to motivate their classmates. It is important to remember that high school students are permanent residents of their community and do not have the problem many college students encounter of being considered "outside agitators." As they are full-time residents, there should be no doubt as to why they are concerned about various environmental, consumer, or other community problems. They can perhaps also team up with community members who have skills or other resources not available to high school students, which they would like to direct towards a concern they have in common. Some high school science laboratories, for example, are sufficiently well-equipped to carry out analyses to discover the most common forms of air and water pollution. If not, high school students can often team up with students at nearby colleges or universities. Not only will this type of program alert a community to the dangers of pollution, but another immediate educational benefit is that testing substances in the students' own environment is more likely to stimulate interest than experiments with packaged samples from science supply houses.

With a little preparation, high school civics students are capable of observing town and city agencies in action and evaluating their performances. These evaluations can be printed and distributed to voters. Some high school students may be old enough to vote, and most will reach eighteen very shortly, so interest and activity in this area by high school students should not be considered premature.

Home economics classes can conduct retail price surveys to compare costs between stores. These same classes can prepare analyses of the nutritional value and labeling of the most commonly purchased foods. Both of these programs have obvious benefits to the community as well as to students who participate in the surveys.

Vocational school students are in a unique position to inspect and evaluate television, appliance, or automobile repair work. Students in other subject areas can undertake similar studies as part of their regular course work or as extracurricular activities.

Teachers benefit from this empirical approach in obvious ways. Many students understandably put little effort into a term paper that will be filed away in a desk drawer or wind up in a wastebasket. But few students will turn out a sloppy piece of work if it is destined to be released to the news media or form a link in a chain of evidence leading to a major investigation or legal action. Schools benefit from this type of research because they are better able to fulfill one of the primary functions of education, performance of public service. Not only would the schools and the students benefit from participating in relevant, experiential learning, but the entire community would benefit from their findings. This is true even though from time to time different members of the community might be offended by a particular project. In addition to the short-run community benefits from each study, there is the long-run benefit of turning out students skilled in the practice of citizenship. This last benefit cannot be overemphasized. It is naïve to think that people who maintain total noninvolvement in community affairs while students will assume responsible citizenship roles upon receipt of a diploma. Citizenship, like any other skill, must be acquired through practice. High school and even junior high school is the time to start practicing.

Organizing the High School

Forming a Public Interest Research Group (PIRG) consisting of full-time professionals supported entirely by high school students is not easy, but it can be done. There are several problems which must be solved before the program can become a reality. In the first place, the student fee collection which gives stability to university PIRGs is not possible in most high schools, although some student association cards could be adapted to the PIRG plan. Second, many high schools have not emerged from the authoritarian structures of the past and are still ruled by the edicts of powerful administrators. Third, community sentiment governs the conduct of high schools to a greater extent than it does colleges and universities, except for community colleges. Community opinion, therefore, can determine the fate of the PIRG, regardless of the merits of the proposal. Fourth, high school students are still caught up in interschool rivalries and look upon their fellow students in the parochial school or the "school across town" as opponents rather than as allies. But to state the difficulties of organizing a high school PIRG is not to imply that the task is impossible.

Along with these obvious disadvantages, high school organizers have several important advantages over college students. First, they are far more numerous (32 million high school students compared to 9 million in college), though this advantage is tempered by the fact that the schools themselves are on the average smaller. Thus, a smaller percentage need participate to achieve success. Second, most high school students live at home and have most of their material needs provided by parents. Allowances or part-time jobs often give them more *disposable* income than college students, many of whom must support themselves. Third, their greater familiarity with and presence in the community enables them to avoid being labeled interlopers. However, no catalogue of theoretical strengths and weaknesses really gives an accurate picture of the situation at a particular school. Only an action program developed by persons who know the particular situation can really gauge this. And while conditions vary greatly from school to school, most obstacles can be overcome by energetic and imaginative students assisted by a few dedicated teachers.

The need for high school PIRGs should be obvious. Until students employ full-time activists to help focus their work and increase its impact, large-scale town, county, or citywide organization is not possible. But multischool organizations cost money and can only be sustained if a way is found to raise funds. There are various possibilities. A special yearly fee can be levied and paid by a slight increase in the cost of school athletic events, plays, or other student government activities. For example, if the price of each football game, basketball game, dance, and play were increased by only 10 cents, most schools would raise several thousand dollars or the equivalent of $3.00 or $4.00 per student. In some schools, student governments receive the proceeds of the vending machines in the cafeteria and lounge areas. It would be a suitable irony to apply the proceeds from candy and Coke toward public interest action programs. Recently, student governments have been active in organizing "marches for hope" or "marches for life" in which students collect $.50 or $1.00 for each mile they walk. A similar march could go a long way toward funding a public interest group. Other schools have used the $5.00 or $6.00 traditionally paid for one night's use of a cap and gown to fund worthwhile activities. Last year in Connecticut, high school students raised almost $40,000 through a combination of cake sales, car washes, concerts, marches, and door-to-door solicitations. This money helped start the Connecticut Citizen Action Group.

The simple fact is that there is plenty of money available to support concerts, games, and other forms of entertainment. A small fraction of this money could immensely aid local communities. If even 1 percent of the energy and money poured into high school football were diverted to public interest research groups, high school students would quickly emerge as a force to be reckoned with in the nation as a whole.

Structure

This initial emphasis on fund raising is not misplaced. Money is what enables students to hire permanent staff without which strong organizations cannot develop. Too often activists ignore structure building to concentrate instead on the more tempting prospect of working on substantive issues. When trying to start a new group this temptation should be resisted, since it almost always leads to a brief flurry of activity which expires when the original activists tire or graduate. Even if the initial enthusiasm can be maintained, summer vacations, holidays, and examination periods hamper the development of strong student action groups. Other hindrances to the formation of a strong group are inexperience, lack of expertise, and the lack of means to obtain a remedy. Without a full-time staff, abuses that investigators uncover may be spotlighted and criticized, but affecting a solution is often impossible. A staff of full-time skilled workers can provide continuity, expertise, and the possibility of solutions through voluntary, legislative, or legal action.

A PIRG will vary in size depending on the size of the support base. A good formula to aim for is a support base of 10,000 to 25,000 high school students at a rate of $4.00 or $5.00 per student per year. This would raise $40,000 to $125,000, enough to support a professional staff and fund student projects. Obviously, effective organizations could be formed with more or less money and greater or fewer participating students. Even a single student "ombudsman" could accomplish a great deal. But for major impact, larger organization is needed.

Because a high school is too small to fund a PIRG by itself, organization must take place on a multischool basis. A simple formula for support and control of the PIRG by a student board can be devised to fit each situation. For example, each school could receive proportional representation on the basis of one representative for each five hundred contributing students. A yearly contribution of $4.00 or $5.00 per student could be set. Each school could employ its own fund-raising techniques so long as the amount agreed upon was collected. Special provisions could be made for schools in low income areas.

The salaries paid PIRG staff members are considerably lower than those the staff would receive working for government or business. Many people are willing to accept substantially lower salaries because of the opportunity to work effectively on public interest problems. A budget of $60,000, for example, would be sufficient to maintain an office with a staff of two lawyers, a scientist, one or two community organizers, and an office manager-secretary. This size staff, managed aggressively, would have the resources students lack to research social problems and the muscle to bring about some solutions.

In states where university PIRGs are already formed, high

school students have the option of combining their efforts with them. Without much difficulty control can be apportioned between high schools and universities by a formula which gives due weight to each participating unit. The same formula later could be used to include nonstudents who wished to contribute to the PIRG. The Vermont PIRG already is operating on this formula with no apparent problems of control.

Projects Suitable for Citizen Action

Not every school is ready to help launch a high school PIRG. In some cases, town or school officials may actively oppose the PIRG plan. In others, students are so apathetic or disorganized that it is impossible to muster enough support to create a multi-school group. Regardless of the problem, where a PIRG cannot be organized, concerned students can still undertake meaningful projects if they are willing to exercise creativity. Obviously these same projects could be undertaken more easily if a PIRG were formed and full-time staff were available to assist student volunteers. Nevertheless, more can be done than is presently the case. For example, numerous high school ecology clubs now devote most of their efforts to recycling drives. Each classroom has a box to collect scrap paper and once a month a truck is hired and the paper is hauled to a central collecting center. Of course, there is nothing wrong with this type of activity, except that with the skills and resources available in the school it is a pathetically small response. If recycling is a principal concern, instead of just collecting paper, it would be far better to get individual schools and eventually entire school districts to recycle their paper and to purchase only recycled paper. This type of recycling program, perhaps coupled with the collection of other used paper, would greatly increase the beneficial impact of an ecology club's effort. If the program proved successful in schools, it could expand to include other public institutions, such as hospitals, government agencies, libraries, and other schools.

Many ecology clubs ignore problems within their own high schools and direct their attention towards the problems of ocean pollution or of the disposal of refuse left on the moon. Before worrying about global issues, it is better to develop and practice techniques to solve small problems within their scope of effectiveness.

In many schools vending machines dispense throwaway cans instead of reusable bottles. Milk is served in half-pint cartons made of paper instead of returnable glass bottles. More serious is the trend to adopt disposables, in school cafeterias, like plastic utensils and paper plates, and to serve precooked food. Each of these situations provides the basis for a useful start-up project.

For example, a concerted drive by students in a single school to ban soda machines dispensing only throwaway cans initially might not make much of an impact on soda manufacturers. But as more schools joined the plan, the force of consumer pressure and the threatened economic loss would help assure the return of the reusable bottle. The same arguments are true regarding milk container use. Milk could be poured from bulk dispensers into washable glasses. The savings in paper cartons would be impressive. The situation with cafeteria disposables is more complicated. Labor costs for food preparation, serving, and cleaning up are high, and a school may claim that disposables and precooked food are the only economically sound alternatives to closing the cafeteria down completely. There are no easy answers to these assertions. For a start, ecology-conscious students should prepare a cost benefit analysis to determine the true cost of cafeteria disposables. Some factors they might consider are the social cost of unemployment of the kitchen staff; the extra cost of garbage disposal; the measurable increase in solid waste due to disposables which will accumulate over a year; and the nutritional value and possible adverse health effects of precooked, prepackaged food.

A victory in one of these small projects can pave the way to a major undertaking later in the year or during the next school year. Once spirit and group solidarity are built up, the group can expand into community projects. It is important to remember that small victories grow into larger ones and techniques that are honed on small projects can later be employed on major issues.

The following projects are more ambitious, but well within the range of competent, motivated high school students.

TELEVISION AND RADIO MONITORING

All television and radio stations broadcast on public airwaves. In order to gain the right to use public property, they must meet certain qualifications and apply for and receive a new license every three years. One requirement that they must fulfill is to prove that they are serving the public interest. Without going into detail, it is sufficient to say that virtually every station, if closely scrutinized, might be found deficient in this area. The following projects merely suggest three areas suitable for citizen action. Each could form the basis of an entire semester's field work. To learn more about these areas and the responsibilities of broadcasting stations, read "Guide to Citizen Action in Radio and TV" by Marsha O'Bannon Prowitt. It is available from the Office of Communications, United Church of Christ, 289 Park Avenue South, New York, New York 10010.

1. How frequently and in what roles do women, blacks, and other minorities appear on television? To answer that question accurately requires several weeks of dawn-to-midnight monitoring of all programs appearing on a particular station. But the results of the study, if they follow the pattern discovered by others, will prove very interesting and may provide the basis, if voluntary action by the station is not undertaken, for a challenge on a license

renewal. At the very least the massive discrimination that almost certainly will be revealed should caution students against unquestioning belief in TV.

The methodology of the study is simple. Standard forms should be prepared with space to list the number of women or minorities that appear and what characters they portray. Special attention should be given to newscasts to determine what portion of the news is devoted to women's affairs or minority news. Students can be divided into teams to perform the monitoring. At the end of the monitoring period, a report should be prepared that would include all of the data that has been gathered, the conclusions arising from it, and the names of the student monitors. The report should be forwarded to the FCC for action when the station applies for its license renewal. The FCC is required to keep a file of all reports received on a station—even comments on post cards— and to consider them at renewal time.

2. Are minority groups represented on the staffs of radio and television stations? The FCC is concerned with more than on-screen appearances of women and minorities. It recently adopted rules which require all stations to develop

> positive recruitment, training, job design and other measures in order to insure genuine equality of opportunity to participate fully in all organizational units, occupations and levels of responsibility in the station.

This means that women must be hired to perform more than secretarial functions and that blacks and other minorities must be *positively* sought after to fill positions at *all* levels of responsibility. In other words, a station cannot point to a full quota of women clerical workers and black janitors as evidence of its affirmative recruiting policies. Nor can it use the defense that no blacks walked in and asked for an executive position. The station itself is obliged to right the employment imbalance. An annual report must be submitted by May 31 detailing statistics on station recruitment and employment of blacks, Orientals, American Indians, Spanish-surnamed Americans, and women.

A civics or social studies class could undertake a project to review the annual reports of all stations within a locality to see if affirmative action were being taken by broadcasters to increase minority employment. This survey would aid in the preparation of a challenge to a station's application for license renewal. It would also teach students about various subtleties of discrimination.

3. Are commercials getting out of hand? Advertisements appear on television with depressing frequency. Fortunately, most adults are capable of erecting mental blocks against their competing claims. But young children have no such defenses, especially when their favorite characters also act as shills for toys, breakfast cereals, candy, records, and other products regularly advertised on Saturday morning TV. The advertisements say "Wonder Bread builds strong bodies twelve ways" or "Wheaties is the breakfast of champions"—to the little child this is proof enough. When these messages are hammered home at the rate of fifteen minutes worth of ads per hour of regular morning television programming, children are virtually defenseless.

Students can perform several valuable functions with respect to children's advertising. First, they can undertake a survey to measure the number and frequency of commercials on Saturday morning cartoons compared to afternoon sports events and prime-time evening shows. Second, they can examine the content of the advertisements. A check on whether the most advertised breakfast cereals are the most nutritious ones would be instructive. Third, students could take this information, if it proved that the ads were promoting unhealthy foods, and petition local stations to permit public service advertising to warn children about the content of the commercials being broadcast. Fourth, they could turn over their report to the Federal Communications Commission. There are also local community information projects—speeches, pamphlets, articles in community newspapers—that could be organized to take the collected information to parents directly.

Each of these projects serves a similar purpose. Not only does it teach students something about the media and the uses and abuses of the airwaves, but it provides a basis for responsible action projects which students can undertake as part of the regular course curricula.

EVALUATING REPAIR WORK

This project is especially suitable for vocational school students, but it can be done by anyone concerned with the plight of the mechanically untutored citizen in an increasingly technological world. Few people have any real idea about how television sets, stereos, major appliances, or automobiles really work. They have no reliable way to evaluate the honesty and quality of the repair work and cost estimates given them by repairers. If the broken item is essential most people will pay almost any price to have it repaired or replaced. Here is where a high school evaluation project can prove useful.

For this project, all that is needed is a television set, stereo, car, or some other appliance in good working order. The evaluation team can then take a television set, for instance, and intentionally damage a single part or replace a working tube or fuse with a burnt one. The set should be examined by a teacher or a *repairer who can be trusted* and certified to be in working order except for the damaged part. The set is brought to a repair shop to get a cost estimate on repair. After receiving the estimate the name and address of the repairer, his cost estimate, and the names of the students who brought the set in should be noted. The set should then be returned to the teacher or trusted repairer to be recertified. This process should be repeated until a significant number of estimates are received. If the disparities between the actual cost of repair and the estimate are large, the information should be compiled in a report listing the name and address of each repairer and his cost estimate. Background material should be used to explain the purpose of the test and the methods used. It can then be released to newspapers, radio, and television; if they do not give it enough publicity, the information can be mimeographed and distributed at churches and shopping centers to warn unwary consumers.

Ambitious students can take this project a few steps further if, when the report is released, it is accompanied by a call for town or city council hearings. The students can appear at the hearings as the principal witnesses, generating more coverage and getting valuable public speaking experience. The purpose of the hearings would be to enact a law licensing repairers, with stiff penalties for fraud and with a provision for city inspection teams to perform, on a full-time basis, the inspection programs the students had initiated. The California law can be used as a model and adapted to fit particular community needs.

EVALUATION OF CITY OR STATE INSPECTION FACILITIES

During the past few years many citizens have become alarmed over environmental deterioration and consumer abuse. In response, a number of cities and states have set up consumer or environmental agencies and passed laws giving these bodies power to regulate the marketplace and to protect the environment. Unfortunately, the best laws are useless, unless they are enforced well. It does no good to give people a right unless they also have the means to enforce that right. Similarly, inadequate inspection provisions make even the best laws unenforceable.

This project can be approached from several directions. Students first could analyze the number of establishments a consumer department is supposed to regulate and then, in light of its inspection staff, determine if regulation is possible. Or a survey could be made to determine whether the inspection was being conducted responsibly. For instance, in the environmental area, an air quality monitoring station in New York City located in Central Park would report radically different readings on carbon monoxide levels than one located in Times Square or in a midtown tunnel. Another approach would be to evaluate the qualifications of the inspectors. How much training do they possess and what equipment do they have at their disposal? How frequent are inspections? Are they announced beforehand? How much time is spent on each inspection? What records are kept? Are they publicly available? A good area to investigate is the quality and frequency of the inspection of restaurants. In many communities, when citizen complaints have brought about strict inspection, some of the best restaurants have been forced to clean up—and in a few cases, close down—until sanitary conditions were brought to an acceptable standard.

This information should be compiled in a report and distributed to city or state officials and to those in charge of the various agencies whose inspection practices were evaluated. If the report reveals shocking abuses, releasing it to the newspapers can prompt establishments to clean up bad conditions simply to avoid future adverse publicity. Students can attempt to find a lawyer who will take the case to court to ensure that the law will be enforced.

There are numerous other projects which high school students can organize. Some are elaborated in Chapter 9, others can be found in the dozens of environmental and consumer books published in recent years. A good source of citizen action projects is *A Public Citizen's Manual for Action* by Donald K. Ross, to be published in early 1973. Once teachers and students begin to think along action lines, suitable projects will not be hard to come by. Many students claim that if only there were something to do they would do it. There is no excuse for such an attitude. There is plenty to do. All that is needed is the energy, courage, and determination to do it.

9 SOME PUBLIC INTEREST PROBLEMS AND SOLUTIONS

When student energy is coupled with professional skills, major changes can be accomplished. There are numerous areas where their efforts may make important differences in the formation of laws, the implementation of laws, the behavior of corporations, the responsiveness of government, and the lives of people. The following projects are offered as suggestions for a student PIRG's action program. Naturally, there are many other projects that will arise from the special circumstances in a state or region.

Some of these projects may also be undertaken by individuals or groups without a PIRG. Not all students are organizers nor are students in every state ready to form a PIRG. Much can be done even where the broad base of a student organization does not exist. Indeed, there are projects that should not be undertaken by a PIRG. Foremost among those is investigation of the universities themselves. A PIRG should direct its energies outward from the campuses to society at large, not only to avoid an "ivory-tower" syndrome, and not only because, in any impartial evaluation of American society, it should be clear that the greater and more pressing problems are off-campus, but also because directing the energies and resources of a PIRG inward to the university is almost sure to destroy the PIRG: (1) few universities will be willing

123

to permit a fee increase to support an organization that may turn against them, and (2) investigation of the university itself will, as experience in non-PIRG cases has often shown, split the student body, destroying the unity of purpose that is essential if the PIRG is to support itself. The PIRG should direct itself to the broad public interest; other groups may focus inward.

In most cases, attempts to do so by reforming an agency or implementing a piece of legislation require long-term efforts that individuals or *ad hoc* groups cannot provide. These attempts may also require litigation or a process of administration action that also requires resources most individuals lack. In these cases, it is essential that a PIRG be available to go the last step that is often most crucial in really affecting the problem.

Property Tax Project

About 85 percent of local tax revenues and about 40 percent of total local revenues come from property taxes. This means that the quality of schools, sanitation, police, health and environmental protection, and other services which a local government can provide depends in large measure upon this one tax.

Property taxes are also important to the "private" business sector. The profitability of a commercial building, a speculative investment in vacant land, and even a large industrial property can be heavily influenced by the level of the property taxes upon it.

The combination of these two forces—the need of the community for tax revenues and the desire of businessmen for maximal profit—can bring an intense pressure to bear upon the administration of the tax. And frequently the administration is not strong enough to withstand it. One leading scholar, Edwin R. A. Seligman, has written ". . . the general property tax as actually administered is beyond all doubt one of the worst taxes known in the civilized world." The tax is commonly administered by elected assessors, untrained and underpaid, who frequently have business and political ties to real estate and business interests in the community. As a result, the social, economic, and political powers in a community quite often leave their footprints upon the administration of the local property tax. The study of the tax is really a window through which to see the use and abuse of other forms of power in local government.

Some particular access points which citizen groups might explore are the following:

CONFLICTS OF INTEREST

Assessment offices and local property tax appeals boards are frequently laden with realtors, real estate developers, apartment building owners, construction company executives, and insurance men. (Zoning boards, it should be noted, are also so constituted.) These men are in a position to use their public office to advance their private business interests. Citizens could study how these men have acted or voted upon properties in which they might have a business interest.

Some states, it should be noted, have conflict-of-interest laws and codes of ethics which prohibit officials from acting in matters in which they have a private financial interest. The New York Attorney General has ruled that under New York law a realtor is barred from acting as local assessor.

INCOMPETENCE AND MALADMINISTRATION

Some assessors have no background or training. They spend little time on their job, rarely reassess properties, and raise assessments only when properties are bought and sold or new buildings are constructed. Assessment records may be kept in an informal manner, and in pencil, so that they can be "adjusted" or changed at whim.

Citizens have a vital stake in the efficiency and competence of property tax administration. It is highly relevant to know how qualified the local assessor is, how he goes about his work, and whether his operating procedures and record-keeping measure up to legal requirements.

EXEMPTIONS

A property tax exemption is a form of hidden subsidy. Prepare a list of all the exempt properties in your community and ask, "Should the people of this community be supporting these property owners?"

Abuse of exemptions fall into two categories. First, exemptions are often granted to those not legally entitled to them. Common examples are income-producing properties of supposedly nonprofit organizations such as churches, clubs, and educational institutions. Check to see if the office building owned by a fraternal organization and rented out to private businesses is exempt from property taxes as a "meeting hall." Or see if the vacant land that churches and schools have been holding for years while it grows in value is off the tax rolls as land used for "educational or religious purposes."

Some exemptions are within the letter of the property tax law but are questionable on other grounds. Is a country club which practices racial or religious discrimination eligible for a state subsidy in the form of an exemption from property taxes?

Granting property tax exemptions to groups that do not really need them constitutes another abuse. In such cases the rich simply get a free ride. In some states "veterans" and "homestead" exemptions erase a good measure of the property tax liability of wealthy home owners. Real estate developers and speculators in land often use so-called "farm land" assessment laws to minimize their tax bills while their land "ripens" for development. Private businesses often ride home free on exempt state- or federally-owned property by leasing it from the government.

126

PUBLIC INTEREST PROBLEMS

Property tax records should be public records, so that citizens can check on the integrity of the assessing and taxing function, and so that taxpayers can determine if they have been treated unfairly and then compile the evidence with which to win a case in court. There are state laws requiring that certain records be kept open to the public.

But frequently local assessors establish little tyrannies over their domains. They create complex procedures which effectively frustrate citizen efforts to see records. They keep the records in a form which no one but they themselves can understand.

It is important, then, to find out what records are and are not available. Ask to see the assessment rolls, the assessor's "work sheets," his tax maps, and the manuals provided by the state detailing the rules he is supposed to follow in establishing values for property. The work sheets are especially important. They show *how* the assessor actually arrived at a given value. Without them, taxpayers have no way of proving that the assessor did not observe the procedures he is legally bound to follow.

Also important are records of reductions and appeals. Is there a record of all such appeals? Is the amount of the reduction given, along with an explanation? If no such records are kept, the assessor and/or the Board of Appeals can dole out assessment reductions at will, without being accountable to legal standards or public scrutiny.

UNDERASSESSMENT

Corruption of the property tax system most frequently appears in the form of underassessment. Sometimes only individual properties are underassessed—the home of a political crony, the business property of a friend or business partner. But at other times whole classes of property are undreassessed. Neighborhoods of white home owners may be underassessed in comparison to neighborhoods where blacks reside, largely because political power resides in the white neighborhood. Large industrial and commercial properties may win underassessments through their economic power or political influence.

Most state constitutions require, in effect, that property be assessed at "full market value" or some variant of that phrase. But courts have held that assessments do not have to be at *full* market value as long as all taxpayers pay an equal percentage of full market value. Thus to prove underassessment, one must show that some property owners are paying a lower percentage of full market value than others are.

Assessed values are fairly easy to determine from the local assessment records. But determining full fair market value may pose problems. Residential property is the easiest to work with. Sales figures are the most reliable standard of full market value, and residential property is bought and sold frequently. With a little ingenuity, students should be able to approximate a rough full market value for almost any residential property and then compare the ratio of the assessed property to the full value on that property (the "assessment ratio") to the ratios for other residential properties in the jurisdiction.

Commercial and industrial properties are harder to work with. They are bought and sold less frequently, and especially in the case of industrial properties, they tend to be unique. Nevertheless, there are ways to approximate full market values. Local realtors and appraisers may be helpful in arriving at estimates. For industrial property, check annual reports, company publicity, and labor union publications to find out how much capital investment has gone into particular plants over particular years. Then see how much the assessment has gone up in those years. In addition, insurance companies often have rules of thumb for estimating the amount of capital investment necessary to produce a given output of goods.

Another approach is to ignore the assessments on buildings and improvements, and work with land values only. Get a tax map from the assessor's office or from a private mapping firm. If the assessment records are broken down between land and buildings, determine the land assessment per square foot of each lot. When the mapping of a particular area is completed, the cases of underassessment should be apparent.

In looking for the underassessments in a community, the patterns to be alert for are favors to political supporters, to particular businesses or to large businesses generally, to politically powerful residential neighborhoods, and to properties in which assessment or local government officials have an economic interest. Vacant land is also often underassessed. Sometimes when improvements are made on vacant land, they do not even appear on the assessor's records.

TAXPAYERS' ORGANIZATIONS

In more than one community, the so-called "taxpayers' organization" has been taken over by the entrenched political and economic powers of the community. Such leadership focuses the group's attention on cutting down local government expenditures —usually for schools—and diverts it entirely from studies of whether everyone in the community is bearing his fair share of the tax load.

It would be a service to the community to lay bare the real nature of the group that is supposed to be serving it. Who are the leaders? What are their business and political connections? Does the leadership observe the group's own bylaws? What issues has the group promoted? What issues has it shied away from?

ACTION FOR A CHANGE

RESOURCE PEOPLE

Resource people have to be chosen from those outside the local "establishment." One or two knowledgeable mavericks can be a tremendous asset. Sometimes even a person within the "establishment" can cooperate secretly. People to look for are lawyers, local government officials, *retired* government officials, candidates defeated in recent elections, realtors, appraisers, newspaper reporters, and the like.

RESOURCE TOOLS

Resource tools include the following: land-use and tax maps, available from the assessor's office or from private mapping and appraisal firms; assessment roles and the assessor's work sheets; deeds; state handbooks for use by assessors; real estate pages of local newspapers; aerial photographs; "People and Taxes," a monthly newspaper, has valuable information regarding taxes. A sample copy is available from the Tax Reform Research Group, 733 15th St. N.W., Washington, D.C.

Perhaps the two most potent resource tools are lawsuits and publicity. Even the promise of these can do wonders.

Occupational Safety and Health Project

Student PIRGs can help workers enforce their rights to a safe and healthful work environment. Each year at least 15,000 workers are killed from work-related injuries; two and one-half million more are disabled, and a total of eight million injured. A recent Department of Labor-sponsored survey indicates that there probably are 25 million injuries each year. No one knows how many diseases really occur but surveys indicate that millions are exposed to excess levels of contaminants which result in shortening of life expectancy and possible long-term harmful effects such as genetic damage or the onslaught of diseases after retirement. The

130

problem of occupational disease is equally serious to that of job injuries. Many workers suffer from the gases, dusts, fumes, and other contaminants they encounter in their work environment. The Department of Health, Education and Welfare estimates at least 390,000 cases of occupational disease each year, but this is acknowledged as only the tip of the problem because many diseases are not officially identified or not reported. Many job injuries are not reported either.

One reason that occupational health and safety is a mounting problem is the rapidity with which new chemicals are introduced into the industrial process. What effects many of these substances have on workers are still unknown. Generally they are presumed safe until proven otherwise. Even in areas where the hazards are known, the problems remain because workers' rights to health and safety have largely gone unrecognized or unenforced.

The Occupational Safety and Health Act passed December 29, 1970, gives workers a means of protection through government standards and enforcement. The Act protects nearly all workers since it covers all businesses having an effect on commerce, except where another federal agency or the Department of Labor has been given statutory authority to carry out its own occupational safety and health programs. At present, this law applies to an estimated 57 million workers and 4.1 million work places.

The Act directs the Secretary of Labor to establish standards for occupational health and safety within two years after passage of the law. Interim but generally inadequate standards are in effect now. The Secretary is also directed to approve plans submitted by states that wish to assume responsibility for development and/or enforcement of standards if they meet the requirements of the Act. At the present time, the Department of Labor's actions in implementing the new law show that the Department is attempting to relinquish its enforcement responsibility to the states without requiring that the states first develop adequate state plans. However, since the federal law requires each state plan to be "at least as effective" as the federal plan, student PIRGs can be very valuable in documenting whether or not state procedures actually comply with Section 18 (c) of the federal Act. The first step in effective student monitoring of the compliance of either state or Federal governments is to acquire a copy of the Federal act. Any deviation from its terms by the Department of Labor or the state should be reported immediately to affected labor unions, if any, and to the Chairmen of the House and Senate Committees on Labor.

The law provides that each covered employer has a general duty to furnish employment free from "recognized hazards" causing or likely to cause death or serious harm to workers, even if such hazards are not covered by a standard. "Serious harm" is broadly defined by the Federal law, so as to include any expected diminution of a worker's life or work life.

The act will not be effective, however, without significant pressure from workers and other citizens for meaningful enforcement. Fortunately, there are a number of ways the public and the affected worker can take part in enforcement of the law. Here is where student PIRGs can be effective.

1. A major problem confronting workers is their inability to identify health and safety hazards. Student PIRGs can set up programs for analyzing dusts from the work environment of a particular plant or industry to identify substances that may be harmful to workers' health. The workers or the union, if any, can authorize the students to collect samples, or can give them product samples for analysis. Research may be done both by professionals on the full-time staff and by students, who may make the research part of a laboratory project.

When hazardous substances are discovered, the results can be used to demonstrate the need for a new standard or amendment of an existing one, through procedures established under the Act. Or an analysis may determine that dust levels in a particular plant exceed the standard and the employer is in violation of the law. Here the Act provides ways for instigating enforcement procedures.

2. A student PIRG can also operate a voluntary service for workers. Part of the service may be devoted to education. For example, the PIRG could teach workers how to use audiometers to measure the noise levels in their work places and document cases where the law is being violated. Since it is often difficult for outsiders to gain access to plants, much of the initial data collection and detection of hazards will be left to workers themselves; however, students can assist workers in developing the best methods to collect data or detect problems. Many students can be found on campus who have worked in unhealthful or hazardous jobs during summers and can lend their knowledge and assistance.

3. A PIRG-organized voluntary service can also test workers for symptoms of occupational disease. Sometimes this will save a worker's health. For example, if textile workers receive regular medical tests they can be warned when they have the early stages of "brown lung," a chronic lung disease caused by breathing cotton dust, and the disease can be arrested. In addition, the test can demonstrate the need for greater protection for workers. Regular medical examinations should be provided by employers, but many fail to do so. Public health or medical students working with individual workers or union locals can set up a testing program. HEW can be contacted for information on safety and health criteria and can also be requested to make investigations and to require the employer to monitor the levels of dangerous substances in the air of the work place.

4. When standards are proposed they will be based on criteria developed by HEW. These criteria are the HEW recommendations as to standards necessary to assure that no employee will

suffer "impaired health, diminished life expectancy or diminished functional capacity" even if he is exposed to the levels recommended for his entire adult working life. Student PIRGs should be prepared to challenge the HEW criteria by submitting evidence and recommendations to HEW before the criteria are finalized, and to initiate HEW action to set criteria. Then, when the Department of Labor appoints advisory committees to set standards, student PIRGs should monitor this process and recommend qualified faculty or community health experts to assure no unjustified weakening of standards. A student PIRG can monitor this process by submitting comments and data to the Secretary of Labor.

Student PIRGs should examine the 1970 Occupational Safety and Health Act, and their own resources, in setting up a program. They may want to challenge a state program where the state is trying to take over enforcement of the Act with an inadequate plan.

The U.S. Department of Labor, Washington, D.C., can provide information on the Act. For information on research into occupational disease, write to the Bureau of Occupational Health, U.S. Department of Health, Education, and Welfare, Washington, D.C. The state AFL-CIO will also have materials and information on enforcing the rights of workers under the Act.

Employment Discrimination

Title VII of the Civil Rights Act of 1964 forbids employment discrimination on grounds of race, sex, creed, or national origin. Executive Order 11246 as amended by 11375 goes a step further and requires all companies doing business with the government to take "affirmative action" to hire women and members of minorities. However, it is safe to say that virtually every major United States corporation violates these laws in one or more ways.

To comply with these Executive Orders, a company doing

business with the government must do more than hire a respectable quota of black janitors and women secretaries. Such an employer must seek out minority groups and women to fill jobs at all levels in the company, including management. The scarcity of women and minorities in middle and upper management positions is testimony to corporate disregard for these laws.

Students can help ensure compliance with civil rights laws in several ways. A single complaint to the Equal Employment Opportunities Commission (EEOC) may generate a major EEOC investigation which will uncover additional instances of employment discrimination.

Many cities and states have Human Rights Commissions that handle similar charges. Students can investigate the employment practices of local banks, construction companies, or department stores. The phone company is often a good place to start. Based on the number of complaints received by the EEOC and the evidence of government investigations, the Bell system is the largest sex discriminator in the country. When discrimination is found, charges can be brought before the local agency or, if satisfaction is not received, the EEOC can be asked to intervene.

Investigations frequently require ingenuity. For example, a group of New York University law students were assured by state officials and construction contractors that blacks accounted for 20 percent of the labor force on construction projects in New York State. The students went to construction sites where they counted the number and noted the color of all workers entering the sites. Their figure of blacks on the labor force turned out to be less than 5 percent. The students' effort resulted in extensive newspaper coverage, temporarily halted construction on one major building site, and forced acceleration in minority hiring programs.

For more information on employment discrimination and citizen remedies, write to the local state employment office or the EEOC, 1800 G Street, N.W., Washington, D.C. 20006.

ACTION FOR A CHANGE

Environmental Projects

Universities in every part of the country, whether urban or rural, are surrounded by symptoms of a deteriorating environment. Near one campus, a factory belches acrid smoke. Another is neighbor to a ticky-tacky urban sprawl, and a third borders an open sewer that once was a trout stream. Air, water, and noise pollution are endemic, and students everywhere can establish effective environmental action programs to combat them. In the past, many environmental groups have been all too willing to take stands on large national issues but reluctant to undertake positive action on serious local problems.

The range of possible action programs is limitless. The following is a capsule list of some possible projects:

WATER POLLUTION

Dumping industrial wastes in a river without a permit from the Army Corps of Engineers violates the 1899 Water Refuse Act. This act requires United States Attorneys to bring suit if unpermitted wastes are being dumped into navigable waters. If the U.S. Attorney does not act, a private citizen is permitted to bring the suit and, when successful, collect half of the total amount the company is fined.

Congressman Henry Reuss, House Office Bulding, Washington, D.C., will send on request a free kit detailing how to bring such a suit. Following his simple instructions, student environmental groups can put a stop to unsanctioned water pollution.

LEAD PAINT POISONING

Chips of lead-base paint are a serious health hazard. Eaten usually by small children, they can lead to brain damage, mental retardation, and, in some cases, death. The problem of lead poisoning from paint is most acute in low-income-area homes. Here, landlords in many cases continue to use paint with large amounts of lead because it is the cheapest paint they can buy. When they

136

switch to better-quality paints for repainting, the problem of lead poisoning remains. Under the new layers of low-lead paint are the many layers of high-lead paint from previous years. When the paint chips and peels, not only the new paint comes off but much of the old. Repainting is not enough.

Students can detect lead in paint chips rapidly and accurately by using equipment available in the chemistry departments of most universities. Where dangerous levels of lead are found, the landlords and tenants should be alerted of the hazard.

Analyses can also detect actual lead poisoning. Detection at an early stage can prevent serious brain damage. Urine, blood, or hair samples are needed for analysis, and students working with public health teams or community clinics can help gather and analyze these samples.

If they find a high correlation between the use of lead-based paints and actual cases of lead poisoning, students can prepare actions against the landlords who permit unhealthy and potentially fatal conditions to exist. They can alert the Housing Authority, prepare legislation, or bring a suit against the worst offenders. For more information write the Medical Committee for Human Rights, Lead Poisoning Project, 710 South Marshfield, Chicago, Illinois 60612.

AIR POLLUTION

In December of 1970, Congress passed the Clean Air Act (Public Law 91-604), the strongest air pollution legislation in its history. In order for this Act to be effective, enforcement must be strong and uncompromising.

The Clean Air Act of 1970 contains four important provisions for controlling air pollution from stationary sources.

1. It authorizes the administrator of the Environmental Protection Agency to establish national emission standards for many basic pollutants.

2. After these standards have been set, no person may construct any new pollution source which will exceed the air quality standards.

3. The administrator of the Environmental Protection Agency may grant a waiver giving a polluter up to two years to comply with the standards if he finds this period necessary for the installation of controls and believes that steps will be taken to protect the health of persons from "imminent endangerment."

4. The Environmental Protection Agency must scrutinize each state's procedure for implementing and enforcing the emission standards for hazardous air pollutants.

Environmental groups can be invaluable in ensuring that these provisions are administered in the public interest. These groups can be especially valuable in watchdogging a state's enforcement plan. If procedures developed by a state are unnecessarily complicated, or if other provisions of the Clean Air Act are ignored, a formal complaint may be filed with the Environmental Protection Agency. The complaint may result in a revision of state standards or a compliance order from the Environmental Protection Agency.

The same watchdog function is necessary to insure that waivers to the pollution standards are only granted to industries which qualify under the Act.

In all, the Clean Air Act can be a powerful tool for cleaning up our fouled air. However, any legislation is only as strong as its enforcement. By monitoring the state and federal agencies responsible for enforcement, environmental groups can take a large step toward cleaner air.

Consumer Action Centers

Most consumers, on some occasion, buy short-weighted meat, defective appliances, poorly constructed furniture, or bad service. They may be victims of fraudulent credit schemes, deceptive advertisements, or cleverly worded warranties. For some, the fraud is perennial and especially serious. The poor, the undereducated, the ignorant, those with language difficulties, migrant workers, the very young, and the very old are most often hardest hit.

To complicate matters, consumer fraud constitutes an unusually complex area of the law. Prosecution is rare and difficult at best. The result creates a morass where the consumer finds it easier to give up than to pursue his rights. Although there may be a number of local agencies already at work for the consumer, few are completely effective, and the problems have grown so massive that a student consumer group has ample opportunity to make a meaningful contribution.

A student consumer action center can handle all types of complaints, or it can specialize in particular areas such as automobile safety or supermarkets. The cost of a center is minimal; the only expenses need be for phone and stationery. Newspapers and radio and television stations ordinarily provide free public service time to advertise the center's programs, and they are often eager to pass along consumer information.

Consumer centers can perform some or all of the following services:

1. Conduct consumer education programs explaining credit costs, unit pricing, comparison shopping, and the like.

2. Research advertising claims, food quality, credit policies, or pricing patterns in rich and poor areas of the city.

3. Investigate warranty claims to see whether they are honored by local automobile dealers.

4. Train consumer advocates to represent consumers in disputes with manufacturers or retailers.

5. Set up a consumer complaint phone number to give individual consumers a means of voicing complaints. All complaints would then be referred to the appropriate governmental agency or investigated by the staff of the center.

6. Organize picketing or other forms of legal last recourse protest against unscrupulous merchants.

7. Develop consumer programs for local radio and television stations.

8. Start a consumer library.

To set up a center, students should seek advice from faculty members or from local consumer protection groups.

Retail Price Comparisons

Most consumers are unable to conduct market surveys to determine comparative prices. Consequently, buying decisions are made with inadequate information or solely on the basis of geographical proximity to a particular store. The store owner, however, is well aware of competitors' prices. Major grocery chains receive competitors' prices through state and federal government market surveys. Other retail establishments receive the same information or have the resources to compile their own surveys. Trade associations help members to exchange price information. Meanwhile, the consumer, unorganized and without extensive resources, is caught in an information gap.

To make rational purchasing decisions consumers need the same information as retailers. Comparative price surveys are one method that will enable the public to pierce through the gimmickry of deceptive marketing techniques to make an impact on the price structure. As it stands, consumers are supposed to compare prices on their own without the benefit of computerized government market surveys. If consumers collected and shared information in some organized fashion, the individual buyer would be placed on a more equal footing with retailers.

A student PIRG has the resources to organize regular consumer price surveys on local or statewide bases. The system would operate in the following way:

1. Students would draw up a representative list of items and

140

survey the prices of those items at major retail outlets and selected neighborhood stores.

2. The lists would be fed into a computer for fast data analysis.

3. The computer output would be a comparison of prices which would reveal not only specific item price differences, but the overall pricing policies of the chain of stores.

The Hawaii state government has funded such a project since April 1969. On Wednesday of each week, the day specials go into effect, paid surveyors of the Hawaii Food Price Study survey eighty-five items in each of twenty-five stores. Results of the survey are printed in Honolulu's Friday morning newspaper, listing store totals for an abbreviated list of forty items. The results also showed which store had the lowest price for each individual item. The survey rekindled vigorous competition in the area, to the point where stores specifically lowered prices on the surveyed items to better their ranking in the survey. To counter these tactics the survey added fifteen items to the list (which then contained seventy items) that changed from week to week, so no store would know exactly which items would be surveyed. The results of this work demonstrated that three new discount chains had prices averaging 9 percent below the established chains, and showed a total price spread of 18 percent from the lowest to highest stores surveyed. Because these facts were published weekly, the major food chains were forced to lower their prices, bringing down the average food cost in Hawaii by 4 percent. During the same period, mainland food prices rose by 2 percent.

Washington, D.C., consumer groups are utilizing a similar system to gather grocery prices. Each Washington surveyor spends about forty-five minutes gathering price information in a single store and phoning in results. The computer tabulates the results in a matter of minutes. In addition to recording price differences on selected items, the Washington survey is programmed to check price differences between inner city and suburban stores, to search for fraudulent practices in advertised specials, and to isolate which store offers the best bargains. By gathering this information on a regular basis, Washington consumer groups hope to hold down prices and to spot effective inflation, which occurs when item size is reduced without a corresponding reduction in price.

The grocery industry lends itself well to price comparisons because prices change week to week. But the methodology of the survey can be used equally well in price surveys of drugstores, appliance dealers, and other retail establishments on a weekly or monthly basis. In addition, surveys of items that are of seasonal interest could be compared when they are most in demand. For example, toys could be priced during the Christmas season.

Price comparisons are only useful if they are widely disseminated. Newspapers, radio and television consumer reports, and consumer newsletters can help to spread the word. Mimeographed handouts may be distributed as well. It is possible that the commercial media will pay for this service, which can offset the cost of computer time.

A package has been developed to help groups organize price comparisons in their own areas. Included in this package is a manual explaining the methods for getting a survey started and the computer program used by the Washington, D.C., survey.

For further information and a copy of these materials contact:

Mark Fredricksen
P. O. Box 19367
Washington, D.C. 20036

10 SOME FINAL THOUGHTS

Successful student-supported research groups should breed similar organizations in the general community. Chapters of the League of Women Voters, for example, could supplement their own efforts by hiring full-time advocates for the public interest. Women, blacks, and Chicanos could organize a PIRG to guarantee their right to equality. Urban residents intent on protecting their right to breathe could form a PIRG to fight air pollution.

The foundations for such efforts already exist. For instance, automobile owners could turn their moribund automobile clubs into advocates for health and safety. Each AAA chapter could hire its own staff of lawyers to protect the consumer and environmental rights of its members.

Unions could devote some fraction of the interest earned by their pension funds to hire doctors who would work for occupational health safeguards. They could also develop group legal services for their members as some unions are contemplating doing.

Lawyers could organize public interest law firms. In New York, Los Angeles, Washington, D.C., and Chicago, young lawyers have taken a first step in this direction. Law councils in each of these cities have been organized to examine public problems.

The next step is for the councils to hire their own staff attorneys.

In some areas, the public interest movement has already started. Sport and commercial fishermen, through the Fishermen's Clean Water Action Project, P. O. Box 10929, Washington, D.C. 20036, are raising money to support a professional team to combat water pollution. Airline travelers have banded together under the Aviation Consumer Action Program, at the same address, which seek to penetrate the maze of airline regulations to secure rights for the passenger and protect his welfare.

Some states have also begun to form citizen-based groups. In the spring of 1970, high school and college students in Connecticut, organized by attorneys from the Washington, D.C., PIRG staff and aided by community groups and individual citizens, raised almost $50,000 from contributions to form the Connecticut Citizen Action Group. Citizen Action has hired a five-member staff, including three attorneys, to press for environmental quality and other public interest issues.

The Ohio Public Interest Action Group (OPIAG), which was formed at about the same time, is using the $85,000 that it raised to hire a staff of eight public interest activists. During its first year OPIAG was directed by Ralph Nader and members of the Washington, D.C., PIRG. Thereafter it operated independently. Individual cities and towns in both Ohio and Connecticut are considering hiring environmental ombudsmen to protect their air and water.

Even with the formation of these groups, however, the public interest movement needs accelerating, and there is plenty of room to expand the student PIRG concept. Presently, student-supported Public Interest Research Groups are operating exclusively on the state level. Yet state legislatures and regulatory agencies are not always the proper forums for action. Frequently, jurisdiction lies with the federal government. In these cases it would be

144

advantageous to have a full-time lobbyist or public interest lawyer in Washington, D.C. Such a full-time representative could monitor the activities of the state delegation as well as press for public interest issues in federal agencies.

Another way to expand the student PIRG concept would be to create a single Washington organization serving the needs of several state-based PIRGs. Each PIRG could contribute to the salary and overhead expenses of one full-time public interest professional. The staff would work on problems common to all states, such as tax reform, federal health and education legislation, social security and welfare measures, and federal environmental and consumer legislation.

There are endless permutations of these plans, but they all rest on the basic recognition that unless citizens become active in the areas where decisions are rendered, those decisions will not be responsive to citizen needs. Rather, they will continue to be made in isolation behind the closed doors of administrative agencies, in executive sessions of public bodies with little or no citizen input, or in corporate board rooms. Until this kind of secrecy can be removed, the person who reads *The New York Times*, votes regularly, and writes an occasional letter to his legislator will never be a match for a full-time lobbyist. Secrecy and hidden processes cater to special interest representatives who have both the expertise and the economic incentive to force access into decision-making arenas. The unheroic, ordinary citizen is closed out, but the formation of student-supported Public Interest Research Groups provides representation for him.

Additionally, PIRGs make possible the emergence of a new class of public citizen—men and women whose full-time employment is in the public interest arena. Each year, college and professional school graduates search vainly for public interest jobs. Unfortunately, few exist. As a result, there is a steady procession of unenthusiastic workers marching from classroom to corporation. PIRGs provide alternative careers for citizen advocates serving the public interest.

The work of the PIRG may change as the mood of the campus shifts and as rotating student directors inject new issues of concern. This movement insures growth, vitality, and relevance. But, though the issues may change, there remains always the continuing need for effective citizen participation to ensure that the governmental and corporate processes are responsive to the public interest.

Appendix 1
Existing PIRGs, 1972

Citizen Action Group
2000 P Street, N.W. 503
Washington, D.C. 20036

PIRG Clearing House
2000 P Street, N.W. 503
Washington, D.C. 20036

*APIRG
1003 E. 6th St.
Tucson, Arizona 85719

*CCAG
57 Farmington Avenue
Hartford, Connecticut 06101
(203) 527-7191
and
1187 Chapel St.
New Haven, Connecticut 06511
(203) 787-7186

*CNYPIRG
129 Stadium Place
Syracuse, New York 13210
(315) 476-5541, ext. 4591

PIRGH (Hawaii)
Wesley Foundation
1918 University Avenue
Honolulu, Hawaii 96822
(808) 531-7831

INPIRG
Indiana Memorial Union
Room 48-H
Bloomington, Indiana 47401
(812) 337-7575

*ISPIRG
P.O. Box 1059
Des Moines, Iowa 50311
(515) 274-3651

*MassPIRG East
Box 162
Chestnut Hill, Massachusetts 01267
(617) 536-7462

*MOPIRG
P.O. Box 8201
St. Louis, Missouri 63108
(314) 361-5137

* Already operating or preparing to hire staff

*MPIRG
3036 University Avenue S.E.
Minneapolis, Minnesota 55414
(612) 376-7554

*NCPIRG
c/o Frances Zwenig
405 Coolidge Street
Chapel Hill, North Carolina
27514
(919) 942-8233

*NJPIRG
32 W. Lafayette
Trenton, New Jersey
(609) 393-7474

*OPIAG
613 Oak Street
Columbus, Ohio 43215
(614) 221-3596
and
344 The Old Arcade
Cleveland, Ohio 44114

*OSPIRG
411 Governor Building
408 S.W. Second Avenue
Portland, Oregon 97204
(503) 222-9641

*PIRGIM
615 E. Michigan Avenue
Lansing, Michigan 48933
(517) 487-6001

*TexPIRG
P.O. Box 7047
Austin, Texas 78712
(512) 471-5704

*VPIRG
26 State Street
Montpelier, Vermont 05602
(802) 223-5221

*WMPIRG
233 N. Pleasant St.
Amherst, Massachusetts 01002
(413) 256-6434

WNYPIRG
Box 70—Norton Hall
Room 361
SUNY at Buffalo
Buffalo, New York 14214
(716) 831-3609

*Public Interest Research
Centre, Ltd.
Munro House
9 Poland St.
London WIV 3DG England

Appendix 2
Sample PIRG Contracts

AGREEMENT

THIS AGREEMENT entered into this 21st day of May, 1971, by and between Carleton College, Northfield, Minnesota (hereinafter called "Carleton"), and MPIRG Organizing Committee, Inc., a Minnesota non-profit corporation (hereinafter called "MPIRG"),

WITNESSETH:

WHEREAS, a substantial majority of Carleton students has requested Carleton to collect from each Carleton student a fee to be turned over to MPIRG;

WHEREAS, Carleton is willing to collect fees from its students as agent for its students, on Condition that MPIRG will assist in disbursing to Carleton students fees collected by Carleton from students desiring refunds; and

WHEREAS, MPIRG is agreeable to the foregoing Condition;

Now, THEREFORE, in consideration of their mutual promises, Carleton and MPIRG agree as follows:

1. Carleton shall, during the two-year period from and after the commencement date fixed under Paragraph 2 hereof, collect at the beginning of each college term from each student registering at Carleton a special refundable $1.00 fee (hereinafter "refundable fee") to be separately itemized on the fee bill and to be collected at the same time as other student fees are collected. Carleton shall turn over to MPIRG all refundable fees collected minus those collected from students desiring refunds.

2. MPIRG shall assist each student who desires a refund of his fee to obtain the same.

3. Carleton's obligation to collect the refundable fees and to pay the same over to MPIRG shall commence at the beginning of the fall,

149

1971, college term if, but only if, the University of Minnesota Board of Regents has approved of the participation by university students in MPIRG through a collection of refundable fees commencing with the fall, 1971, term. Should the approval by said Board of Regents occur at a date later than the beginning of the fall, 1971, college term, then Carleton's obligation shall accordingly be postponed. Carleton shall be under no obligation whatever under this contract in the event that the Board of Regents of the University of Minnesota do not so approve of the participation by its students in MPIRG by action taken on or before March 15, 1972.

4. Carleton's activities in the collecting of the refundable fees and turning the same over to MPIRG shall be that of a collection and refunding agent only, it being understood: that none of Carleton's own funds shall be paid over to MPIRG pursuant to this agreement; that no refunds paid over to Carleton by MPIRG shall be retained by or inure to the benefit of Carleton; and that neither the execution of this contract nor any performance hereunder shall be construed as approval by Carleton of any action taken or proposed by MPIRG.

5. MPIRG will submit a report on the operations of the collection and refunding system for review by the Carleton Board of Trustees at its spring meeting, 1972.

MPIRG

ORGANIZING COMMITTEE, INC.

By _____

     Its Signatory Agent

Date _____

By _____

     Its Secretary

CARLETON COLLEGE

By _____

     Its President

Date _____

150

AGREEMENT

THIS AGREEMENT entered into this 9th day of July between Macalester College, St. Paul, Minnesota, (hereinafter called "Macalester"), and the Minnesota Public Interest Research Group, a Minnesota non-profit corporation (hereinafter called "MPIRG").

WITNESSETH:

WHEREAS, a substantial majority of Macalester students has requested Macalester to collect from each Macalester student a fee to be turned over to MPIRG;

WHEREAS, Macalester is agreeable to act as a collecting agent for such fees on condition that MPIRG will return fees to students desiring refunds; and

WHEREAS, MPIRG is agreeable to the foregoing condition;

NOW, THEREFORE, in consideration of their mutual promises, Macalester and MPIRG agree as follows:

1. Macalester shall during the two year period starting September, 1971, collect at the beginning of the first college term from each student registering at Macalester a special $3.00 fee. This fee shall not be imposed on students who are receiving $3,000 or more in student financial aid from Macalester during each respective year. Macalester shall turn over, on October 1 of each year, all special fees collected of this contract.

2. Macalester shall collect the fees and pay them over to MPIRG for the yearly periods commencing as stated in the above paragraph.

3. Macalester's activities in collecting fees for MPIRG shall be that of a collection agent only, it being understood that none of Macalester's own funds will be paid over to MPIRG pursuant to this agreement.

4. MPIRG will reimburse Macalester for the actual out-of-pocket expenses (including employee's time) incurred in collecting and handling funds for MPIRG, not to exceed $500.

MPIRG

MACALESTER COLLEGE

_____

By its President

_____

By its Vice President for Financial Affairs

_____

By its Secretary

Appendix 3
Excerpts from an Opinion of the
Attorney General of Pennsylvania

3. *The University of Pittsburgh Has the Authority to Enter Into the Proposed Contract with PIRG*

The University of Pittsburgh is "an instrumentality of the Commonwealth" and is recognized as a "State-related institution of the Commonwealth system of higher education." 24 P.S. §2510–202. The provisions of the act establishing the University of Pittsburgh as a State-related institution provide also that the University shall continue as a corporation for the same purposes for which it had been incorporated and with the same rights and privileges. 24 P.S. §2510–203.

It is unquestioned that the primary purposes of the University of Pittsburgh are educational. In order to accomplish its purposes the University has traditionally engaged in incidental activities which are not intrinsically educational, as that term is usually defined, but which are necessary to, or encourage its academic community to engage in, the principle activities of teaching students and exploring the frontiers of knowledge.

The law clearly recognizes the importance of colleges and universities engaging in activities incidental to the educational process. Moreover, in view of the dearth of authority in Pennsylvania, these powers have rarely, if at all, been questioned in this State. There is, of course, persuasive authority from other states supporting the authority of the University of Pittsburgh to enter into and perform the proposed contract.

The Supreme Court of Oklahoma, in ruling that collection of mandatory fees from students to underwrite construction of an autonomous, student operated union building was within the authority of the Board, stated:

> ". . . 'The board of regents have implied power to do everything necessary and convenient, where it is not prohibited, either express or implied by law, to accomplish the objects for which the institution was founded.'

Under that rule we are not required to look for grants of power to the Board of Regents of the University, but for limitations on its power, in order that we may determine whether or not the act of the defendants . . . has been prohibited. Our attention has been called to no legislative enactment prohibiting the Board . . . from requiring the payment of fees . . . ."

Rheam v. Board of Regents, 161 Okla. 268, 18 P.2d 535, at p. 539 (1933).

The rule cited above has invariably been followed in other states. See *Villyard v. Regents,* 204 Ga. 517, 50 S.E. 2d 313 (1948) (acquisition and operation of commercial laundry by the University even when a number of its patrons were not students or employees of the University was within authority of University); *Long v. Board of Trustees,* 24 Ohio App. 261, 157 N.E. 395 (1926) (operation of student bookstore, held: absent express statutory prohibition, the activity was within the power of the University) and *Iowa Hotel Association v. Board of Regents,* 253 Iowa 870, 114 N.W. 2d 539 (1962) (construction of hotel facility to house campus visitors held to comport with educational objectives). Other cases have permitted construction and operation of metered parking ramp;[1] football fields and stadia,[2] agricultural testing stations,[3] a president's house,[4] an infirmary,[5] and a heating plant.[6]

A search of Pennsylvania law has revealed no express or implied prohibition against educational institutions contracting with student sponsored organizations to collect voluntary fees. In view of the generally accepted rule enunciated by the cases cited above, it is within the power of the University to execute and perform the proposed contract.[7]

---

[1] *Black v. Mossman,* ———— Iowa ————, 170 N.W. 2d 416 (1969)

[2] *Glover v. Sims,* 121 W. Va. 407, 3 S.E. 2d 612 (1939), *Moye v. Board of Trustees of Univ. of So. Carolina,* 255 So. Car. 46, 177 S.E. 2d 137 (1970)

[3] *State* ex rel. *Bushee v. Whitmore,* 85 Neb. 566, 123 N.W. 1051 (1909)

[4] *Cincinnati v. Jones,* 16 Ohio Dec. 343

[5] *Davie v. Board of Regents,* Univ. of Cal., 66 Ca. 693, 227 P.243 (1924)

[6] *Application of Regents of Univ. of Oklahoma,* 200 Okla. 442, 195 P2 936 (1948)

[7] The only statutory authority remotely relevant to this question *permits* a non-profit corporation to charge "school fees" to the extent necessary to accomplish its purposes and to make incidental profits thereon. 15 P.S. §7309.

It is also unquestioned that an intended beneficiary of the contract is a student sponsored activity, a result clearly related to the educational purposes of the University. Moreover, in light of the truly intellectual and educational content of PIRG projects, it can be persuasively argued that execution and performance of the contract is an integral part of the University's academic pursuits.

Finally, it is necessary to address certain points raised in a letter dated February 18, 1972, from J. Tomlinson Fort, Esquire to Dr. George O. Luster, Treasurer of Carnegie-Mellon University. This Department has been advised that some of the points raised in that letter have created concern as to the propriety of a contract between PIRG and the University of Pittsburgh. We have studied the letter with care and, as set forth above, researched the question of the authority of the University of Pittsburgh to contract with PIRG. We find that the authorities cited in the letter do not support the view that an educational institution such as Carnegie-Mellon University or the University of Pittsburgh are without power to contract with PIRG.

The cases principally relied on in the letter are *Stringer v. Gould,* 64 Misc. 2d 89, 314 N.Y.S. 2d 309 (Sup. Ct., Albany Co., 1970) and *Lace v. University of Vermont* (Court of Franklin Co., Vermont, October 15, 1971). *Stringer* involved the question of whether the Board of Trustees of The State University had retained sufficient controls over a fund created by collection of *mandatory* student activities fees. The Court found that a student could not register or be enrolled in classes unless he paid the fee and, if the fee were unpaid by the end of the semester, the student would not receive his grades or degree, if such were the case. The Court held, in light of the mandatory nature of the fee, that the Board of Trustees would be required to determine in advance whether expenditures of the fund were for the purposes for which the fund was created.

In *Lace* as summarized in the letter, the issue again appears to be the extent of control by the Board of Trustees over funds generated by collection of a *mandatory* student activities fee. This analysis was confirmed when this Department had the decision in the *Lace* case read over the telephone by the Clerk of the Court in Vermont. According to the Clerk, students had brought suit challenging collection and expenditure of "student association" fees by the University. Refusal or failure to pay the fee barred a student from matriculating. It appears also that the students were objecting to the use of a large portion of the fee collected to support radical political activities and the failure of the Board to make the student association accountable for its expenditures.

These cases are clearly distinguishable on two important grounds. Firstly, as explained in detail by the spokesman for PIRG, the dues collected for PIRG by the University are not mandatory. Advance notice is to be given, at cost to PIRG, to all students that they need not pay the PIRG dues.

If a student pays and changes his mind after registration or pays inadvertently, sufficient notice and time will be given for him to request a refund. PIRG has not asked and will not ask the University to impose sanctions for non-payment as in *Lace* and *Stringer.*

Secondly, the contract calls for a year-end accounting by PIRG to the University and an audit, at cost to PIRG, if the University deems it necessary. Additional accounting mechanisms, for example semi-annual or even quarterly statements by PIRG, most likely can be negotiated. It appears in *Lace* and *Stringer* that no such accountability was present. . . .

4. *The Proposed Contract Will not Affect the Tax Exempt Status of the University of Pittsburgh*

The question has been raised, at least in connection with student PIRGs in other states, as to whether a university's performance of a contract with a PIRG will jeopardize the university's tax exempt status.

Admittedly, some of PIRG's activities will involve lobbying for the passage or defeat of legislation. In view of these activities, Western Pennsylvania PIRG is applying to the Internal Revenue Service for exempt status under Section 501(c)(4) of the Internal Revenue Code, a provision which provides recognition to "social welfare"-type organizations which may have legislative objectives but which do not engage in partisan political efforts.

Of importance also to the question of tax exempt status is the provision in the Articles of Incorporation of Western Pennsylvania PIRG prohibiting the organization from engaging in any partisan political activity. There are statements in the December 30, 1971, proposal which reiterate this policy.

APPENDICES

The University of Pittsburgh derives its charitable exemption from Federal taxation pursuant to Section 501(c)(3) of the Internal Revenue Code of 1954, as amended. That Section reads as follows:

> Corporations, and any community chest, fund, or foundation, organized and operated exclusively for religious, charitable, scientific, testing for public safety, literary, or educational purposes, or for the prevention of cruelty to children or animals, no part of the net earnings of which inures to the benefit of any private shareholder or individual, no substantial part of the activities of which is carrying on propaganda, or otherwise attempting, to influence legislation, and which does not participate in, or intervene in (including the publishing or distributing of statements), any political campaign on behalf of any candidate for public office.

The regulations under the foregoing provision set out in greater detail the organizational and operational tests by which such an organization will be judged as to its tax exempt status. Regulation Section 1.501(c)(3)–(1)(b)(3), under the heading "Authorization of Legislative or Political Activities," states that:

> An organization is not organized exclusively for one or more exempt purposes if its articles expressly empower it—(i) to devote more than an insubstantial part of its activities to attempting to influence legislation by propaganda or otherwise; or (ii) directly or indirectly to participate in, or intervene in (including the publishing or distributing of statements), any political campaign on behalf of or in opposition to any candidate for public office; or (iii) to have objectives and to engage in activities which characterize it as an 'action' organization as defined in paragraph (c)(3) of this Section.

Regulation Section 1.501(c)(3)–(1)(c) describes the operational tests to be applied in evaluating the status of such organizations. Sub-section 1 of the foregoing Section of the Regulations states that:

> An organization will be regarded as 'operated exclusively' for one or more exempt purposes only if it engages primarily in activities which accomplish one or more such exempt purposes

specified in Section 501(c)(3). An organization will not be so regarded if more than an insubstantial part of its activities is not in furtherance of an exempt purpose.

Subsection 3 of the same Regulation Section defines "action" organizations as follows:

(i) An organization is not operated exclusively for one or more exempt purposes if it is an "action" organization as defined in subdivisions (ii), (iii), or (iv) of this subparagraph.

(ii) An organization is an "action" organization if *a substantial part of its activities is attempting to influence legislation by propaganda or otherwise.* For this purpose, an organization will be regarded as attempting to influence legislation if the organization—

(a) Contacts, or urges the public to contact, members of a legislative body for the purpose of proposing, supporting, or opposing legislation or

(b) Advocates the adoption or rejection of legislation.

The term "legislation," as used in this subdivision, includes action by the Congress, by any State legislature, by any local council or similar governing body, or by the public in a referendum, initiative, constitutional amendment, or similar procedure. An organization will not fail to meet the operational test merely because it advocates, as an insubstantial part of its activities, the adoption or rejection of legislation.

(iii) An organization is an "action" organization if it participates or intervenes, directly or indirectly, in any political campaign on behalf of or in opposition to any candidate for public office. The term "candidate for public office" means an individual who offers himself, or is proposed by others, as a contestant for an elective public office, whether such office be national, State, or local. Activities which constitute participation or intervention in a political campaign on behalf of or in opposition to a candidate include, but are not limited to, the publication or distribution of written or printed statements or the making of oral statements on behalf of or in opposition to such a candidate.

(iv) An organization is an "action" organization if it has the following two characteristics: (a) its *main or primary objective or objectives* (as distinguished from its incidental or secondary objectives) may be attained only by legislation or a defeat of proposed legislation; and (b) it advocates or campaigns for the attainment of such main or primary objective or objectives *as distinguished from engaging in nonpartisan analysis, study, or research and making the results thereof available to the public.* In determining whether an organization has such characteristics, all the surrounding facts and circumstances, including the articles and all' activities of the organization, are to be considered. [Emphasis added by Attorney General.]

Regulation Section 1.501(c)(3)–1(d)(3) defines "educational" as specified in Section 501(c)(3) of the Code as relating to "(a) the instruction or training of the individual for the purpose of improving or developing his capabilities; or (b) the instruction of the public on subjects useful to the individual and beneficial to the community." The definition is rather constricted, but its application cannot be and has not been so treated.

The foregoing statutory provisions have been extensively quoted for the purpose of making absolutely clear that the University of Pittsburgh in and of itself clearly falls within the definition of, and qualifies as, an educational organization exempt from taxation under Section 501(c)(3)—and to which contributions are deductible. It is the loss of such status that is presently feared by execution and performance of the proposed PIRG contract by the University.

Several questions immediately arise from an examination of the above quoted provisions which bear on the question of the University's tax exempt status.[8]

At the threshold, are PIRG's contemplated legislative activities, which may be the final chapter of a lengthy process of problem identification, analysis, and solution, "attempts to influence legislation" within the

---

[8] It must be conceded, in view of the prohibition in The Articles of Incorporation by PIRG and repeated policy statements that no partisan political activity will be undertaken, that the University will not be in violation of the absolute prohibition against any such activity.

meaning of that phrase in the statute and regulations? A persuasive *argument* can be made that PIRG's legislative activities, which will only occur in those instances when the most rational solution to a problem appears to warrant legislative action, are the end product and an integral part of what is an "educational" exercise. If such is the case, there can be no question of the University's status being affected by PIRG's activities.

Secondly, there is the question, in view of the arms-length relationship between PIRG and the University as formalized by the proposed contract, as to whether the activities of PIRG, assuming they are not deemed purely "educational," can be attributed to the University. Guidance on this point comes from the American Council on Education which, in June, 1970, issued "guidelines" for use by its members (1,563 colleges, universities, and educational associations).

The guidelines were prepared and distributed in order to make "educational institutions benefiting from the tax exemption . . . aware of the problem [i.e., activities which would bring into serious question the entitlement of a college or university to tax exemption] and exercise care to make certain that their activities remain within the limits permitted by the statute." The guidelines were issued shortly after the Cambodian invasion protests, and at a time when universities were rearranging calendars to permit students and faculty to engage in political activities, as well as during a time of great political concern and activism on the nation's campuses.

The guidelines pinpoint the focus of the problem as follows:

> Exemption of colleges and universities from Federal income taxes is dependent upon their qualifying as institutions organized and operated *exclusively* for religious, charitable or educational purposes described in Section 501(c)(3) of the Internal Revenue Code. For some years that section has provided that "no substantial part of the activities of " an exempt institution may be "carrying on propaganda, or otherwise attempting, to influence legislation" and further, that an exempt institution may "not participate in, or intervene in (including the publishing or distributing of statements), any political campaign on behalf of any candidate for public office."

By the Tax Reform Act of 1969, the last-quoted prohibition

was incorporated in companion provisions of the Internal Revenue Code dealing with the deduction of contributions for income, gift and estate tax purposes. As interpreted, this provision would deny exempt status to institutions engaging in legislative activities which are *substantial* in the light of all the facts and circumstances. Additionally, it *absolutely* proscribes participation in or intervention by an exempt institution in any "political campaign on behalf of any candidate for public office."

The guidelines go on to make the following statements, all of which are no doubt being relied upon by those resisting the present proposal:

Educational institutions traditionally have recognized and provided facilities on an impartial basis to various activities on the college campuses, even those activities which have a partisan political bent, such as for example, the Republican, Democratic and other political clubs. This presents no problem. However, to the extent that such organizations extend their activities beyond the campus, and intervene or participate in campaigns on behalf of candidates for public office, or permit nonmembers of the university community to avail themselves of university facilities or services, an institution should in good faith make certain that proper and appropriate charges are made and collected for all facilities and services provided. *Extraordinary or prolonged use of facilities, particularly by nonmembers of the university community, even with reimbursement, might raise questions.* Such organizations should be prohibited from soliciting in the name of the university funds to be used in such off-campus intervention or participation. [Emphasis added by the Attorney General.]

As is clear, the distinctions are very fine, if ascertainable at all. The section of the guidelines just quoted does not specifically prohibit the activities suggested here, nor does it clearly indicate that such activity would, in and of itself, constitute prohibited activity on the part of the university. Moreover, the guidelines have only been informally approved by the IRS and it is not clear that the rule set forth concerning prolonged activity was specifically reviewed by the IRS.

Finally, the question remains, even if the PIRG activities are not deemed "educational" and are attributed to the University, are such activities "so substantial" as to bring the University within the proscriptions of §501(c)(3) and the regulations thereunder.

There is case authority, which states that 5% or less of the time and effort of the tax exempt organization devoted to legislative activities is not substantial. In *Seasongood v. Commissioner,* 227 F.2d 907 (6th Cir. 1955) a deduction was allowed with respect to a contribution to a nonpartisan "good-government" organization which supported specific legislation and candidates on certain occasions. The court was clearly influenced in its decision by the fact that so little of the organization's "time and effort," however defined, was devoted to legislative activity in relation to all of its other exempt purpose activities. Similarly, the guidelines of The American Council of Education speak in terms of "substantial in light of all the circumstances."

Under either test it is clear that the PIRG activities would not rise to the level of "substantial" legislative involvement. Firstly, not all of the projects undertaken by PIRG will involve legislative activity. Only those problems under study by PIRG, the solution to which most rationally lends itself to a legislative approach, will prompt legislative activity. Consequently only a percentage (and most probably not a considerable percentage) of the PIRG resources—the proposal of December 30, 1971, contemplates a total budget of $211,690—might be devoted to legislative activity. Viewing this allocation of resources against the total plant, capital, and endowment of the University or its operating budget requires the conclusion that whatever legislative activities are attributed to the university, they are *de minimis* in the context of the University's allocation of resources to other activities. The attribution itself is subject to question, both since PIRG will be paying for the services called for in the proposed contract, and because PIRG will not characterize any of its activities as being those of the University.

Other measures to test substantiality may be suggested, such as a comparison of the total dues (no more than $72,000 in one year) collected for PIRG as against the total fees and charges, including tuition, collected by the University.

By any measure the University's efforts can not be deemed "substantial" for purposes of the Regulations previously cited.

APPENDICES

On the basis of the foregoing, the University has the authority to enter into the proposed contract with PIRG and its tax exempt status will not be affected by any such contract.

Respectfully submitted,

J. Shane Creamer
Attorney General
Department of Justice
Commonwealth of Pennsylvania

Appendix 4
Guidelines for Speakers and Petitioners

1. Know the PIRG program inside out. Read all materials thoroughly, particularly *Action for a Change*. If you have any doubts or questions, resolve them before attempting to speak or petition on behalf of the program.

2. Work with other PIRG people in small group sessions until you feel capable of making a strong presentation. Use role-playing techniques to expose any weaknesses and to sharpen your approach. Subject the whole program to close critical scrutiny.

3. Develop your own style and format. Don't try to memorize a set speech or to imitate someone else's approach. Vary your presentation enough to keep it spontaneous and fresh.

4. Anticipate objections, questions, and criticisms, and be able to respond to them effectively.

5. Avoid a defensive, apologetic stance. You're not asking people to do you any favors by signing the petition.

6. In dealing with resistance, try to distinguish between genuine philosophical or practical objections on the one hand and convenient rationalization on the other. Make your counterarguments responsive to the individual's particular criticism or opposition.

7. Set realistic daily and weekly quotas for signatures, and then make every effort to meet them.

8. Talk specifics. People have difficulty relating to generalities. Read periodicals and papers to stay up on current local and national issues, and connect these issues to PIRG.

9. Avoid a hard sell. Most individuals will recognize the value of PIRG if the idea is intelligently presented to them. Don't collect signatures indiscriminately or attempt to railroad people into signing. Be sure the concept is clearly understood before soliciting a signature.

10. Be familiar with other PIRGs and what they have done. Cite specific examples.

11. Be on the lookout for new recruits. Anyone who manifests some interest should be put to work immediately on petitions, publicity, whatever.

12. Make it easy for people to get to you. The PIRG campaign should be highly visible and accessible. Everyone connected with the organizing effort should be readily identifiable; buttons, armbands, etc., are a help.

13. Demonstrate your conviction, but don't make extravagant, unrealistic claims. Students are justifiably skeptical about wild promises and catch-all instant solutions to complex social problems. Hence PIRG is probably best represented in terms of opportunity or potential.

Appendix 5
Sample Organizing Material

QUESTIONS AND ANSWERS ABOUT ISPIRG
The Iowa Student Public Interest Research Group

ISPIRG FACT SHEET

Rationale:

The Iowa Student Public Interest Research Group (ISPIRG) will be a nonpartisan, nonprofit corporation designated to express the views of college students in Iowa in regard to decisions which effect social change.

General areas of ISPIRG concern, for example, will include environmental issues, delivery of health care, sexual and racial discrimination, housing problems, and consumer protection. The ultimate goal of ISPIRG will be to implement the changes and reforms which its research indicates are necessary. The achievement of this goal will be the product of the combined efforts of students and a full-time professional staff.

When expressing its view, ISPIRG will strictly avoid mere opinion unsupported by facts. ISPIRG will strive for objectivity in its research and recommendations. In sum, ISPIRG will provide an effective vehicle for a student role in the decision-making processes that shape the quality of life.

Funding and Structure:

ISPIRG will be financed by assessing regularly enrolled students three dollars per school year ($1.50 per semester or $1.00 per quarter) at schools where a majority of students have petitioned to establish a local board. Students who choose not to support ISPIRG will be entitled to a full refund of their ISPIRG assessment shortly after the beginning of each quarter or semester.

Students on each campus will elect a local ISPIRG board. Local boards will solicit the cooperation of students, faculty, and groups outside the academic community when setting priorities and carrying on necessary research. In addition, local boards will elect from their membership

167

a statewide ISPIRG board of directors. The statewide board of directors will determine policy, allocate funds, and hire and direct the professional staff.

Educational Role:

Many college students and their schools are currently attempting to render their educational process more relevant to the world outside the academic community. ISPIRG will contribute to this objective by providing an opportunity for students to participate in ISPIRG research projects. In this way ISPIRG will strive to facilitate the application of the reservoir of resources and talent within the academic community to the needs of society as a whole.

GENERAL

What Is a Student-Supported Public Interest Research Group?

Students from public and private colleges and universities in a state, by joining together and taxing themselves one dollar per quarter, can raise sufficient funds to support an interdisciplinary full-time staff to work with them on consumer, environmental, and other problems which affect all citizens of the state.

How Did the Concept of Student-Funded PIRGs Originate?

In response to student queries as to how they might effectively work to solve problems facing all citizens, Ralph Nader suggested that student-funded and -directed public interest research groups were one way in which students could focus their idealism, manpower, and energy for effective change. Such groups build upon lessons learned from past student efforts to effect change and attempt to provide direction, continuity, and expertise vital to effective solution of today's problems.

Why Is There a Need for PIRGs?

In recent years it has become increasingly apparent that the interests of the average citizen in preserving his life support system, eliminating poverty and malnutrition, and encouraging fair practices in the marketplace have been frequently ignored by decision makers. These interests will continue to be neglected in decision-making until:

1) private economic decisions which have an impact on the public welfare are thoroughly studied and discussed;

168

APPENDICES

2) government policy takes into consideration the views and needs of more groups in society; and
3) new methods are developed to ensure consideration of the public interest in private economic decisions and government policy. The move to give voice and power to these long-range concerns of the average citizen is the purpose of the public interest research group.

Why Should Students and Not Some Other Group Be Approached?
It is clear that students, as a group, have fewer vested interests at stake in attempting to solve problems of public concern than do other groups. It is often students who are most able to view problems and evaluate alternative solutions from an unbiased perspective.

What Relation Do PIRGs Have with Existing Consumer and Environmental Groups?
One of close cooperation. There are so few groups existing which are equipped with even minimum resources to articulate and represent the public interest, it is vital that there be no repetition or duplication of efforts.

There will be a sharing of information turned up in research projects. ISPIRG, by exploring ways in which the citizen's voice will be heard and heeded in public and private forums, will help point the way for other groups to affect decision-making.

Finally, there will be close coordination of efforts to implement research findings.

ISPIRG STATEWIDE

Who May Participate in ISPIRG?
Any community college or university in the state is eligible to participate in ISPIRG. Institutions which adopt the ISPIRG method of financing will be entitled to send a delegate or delegates to the Student Board of Directors, to establish local ISPIRG boards on their campuses, and to participate in ISPIRG activities.

Will There Be a Place for the Non-Student Community?
Yes. Community members may donate funds to ISPIRG, but the student board will decide how this money is to be spent.

169

A valuable contribution to ISPIRG activities will come from the community professionals and citizens who donate their time and talents assisting students with particular legal or other specialized needs, and volunteers who can provide liaison with, and outreach to, various community groups.

Additionally, a local ISPIRG board could provide manpower to sympathetic non-student organizations to assist with research efforts, community surveys, or other projects directed toward identifying and solving citizen interest problems in the community.

An effective coalescence of efforts by the ISPIRG boards and community organizations working on a particular problem would provide a formidable voice for the underrepresented, non-private, non-vested interests of the community citizenry. The degree to which ISPIRG becomes involved with the community as a whole will be decided by the local and state boards. It is anticipated that this type of involvement will be quite extensive.

FUNDING

How Will ISPIRG Secure Operating Funds?

ISPIRG will be a student-funded organization, financed by the collection of $1 per quarter or $1.50 per semester from each regularly enrolled student at participating colleges, universities, and community colleges in the state. Students will petition the administration of their school to serve as a collecting agent for the ISPIRG fee.

How Much Money Will ISPIRG Have?

If the petitioning is successful on all eligible campuses, students could raise nearly $300,000 as annual funding for ISPIRG.

Will All Students Have to Pay $1 to Support ISPIRG?

No. At colleges and universities where students indicate by absolute majority on petitions their willingness to support ISPIRG, and where the regents or trustees agree to collect the fee, a refund mechanism will be provided by ISPIRG. Any student not wishing to contribute to the ISPIRG organization can get his or her $1.00 back. The refund rate in states having established PIRG organizations has been less than one percent.

APPENDICES

Why Should a Registration Assessment Be Used, Rather Than Periodic Solicitation of Individual Contributions?

The kind of continuing effort needed to fight persistent problems cannot be sustained without an automatic fund-generating system. *Both continuity and a measure of certainty are needed to attract skilled public interest professionals.* Problems requiring lengthy action must be afforded ample time and resources for solution. A stable monetary base will also allow various short-range projects a chance to develop, while more involved long-range projects are also pursued.

How Will the Money Be Used?

ISPIRG will employ a full-time staff of professionals from various disciplines, such as law, engineering, economics, and other social and physical sciences. Funds will be used to pay their salaries, provide office space and administrative overhead costs. Additionally, a portion of the funds collected will be allocated to the campus chapters for their operating costs in conducting research projects. Further, a contingency fund will be maintained to finance special grants to member campuses for the conduct of particular projects which the Board of Directors deem significant. Funds will also be used to finance publications, court actions, use of consultants, and other costs of specific actions taken by the staff to address a problem.

STRUCTURE AND ISSUES

The ISPIRG organization consists of three principal operating components.

First, and most basic to the organization, are the Campus Boards. Each school in the state which participates in ISPIRG will select a local Board. Any student may take an active role in ISPIRG research and project activities at his or her school.

The Student State Board of Directors is made up of delegates from the local boards. The Board acts as the governing body of the statewide organization.

The third organizational element is the Professional Staff, composed of lawyers, engineers, urban planners, and other physical and social scientists.

Can There Be Any Non-Student Local or State Board Members?

No, only students can serve as board members. ISPIRG will be controlled totally by students. Student funded-Student controlled.

How Will the Staff Be Selected?

Once the funds are collected and the state Student Board of Directors is formed, the Board will determine the initial staffing needs of ISPIRG; in large part the composition and size of the staff will depend on the amount of funds available for maintaining a full-time professional staff.

Through the use of classified ads and other available media, the Board will solicit applications for positions and determine the salaries to be offered. The Board will apply merit principles in the selection process, and all staff will be hired under full usage of equal opportunity principles.

The Board will not only be hiring professionals from diverse disciplines, but will also be looking for a staff composed of a cross-section of racial, cultural, and ethnic backgrounds.

What Is the Relationship Between the Campus Boards and the Students State Board of Directors?

Each delegate to the State Board will provide a crucial informational link between the local organization and the state body. Problems identified locally, either on campus or in the community; research activities of member chapters; and the status of campus project work will be transmitted to the State Board via the delegates.

Delegates will inform the local chapters of staff activities, research efforts of other campuses, and the substantive issue priorities established by the State Board.

Delegates will also be the vehicle for requesting from the board assistance by staff members on particular local research or for obtaining special grant funds for a project that a campus board is doing and for which they need additional monies.

All meetings of the State Board are open and a student member of a local board may attend any meeting. The Board will also call on individual local project leaders for reports and local campus boards can request that the State Board hear a student research proposal.

172

APPENDICES

What Is the Relationship Between the State Board and the Full-Time Staff?

Essentially the staff is the full-time working arm of the students. The State Student Board will hire and fire the staff and will determine their salaries. The Board will determine the priority issues of ISPIRG, and the staff will also provide guidance and input to the Board regarding specific issues or areas of crucial or immediate importance. The staff will report on its work and status of research, legal, or other action activities to the Board at each regular meeting. The staff will be fully accountable and responsible to the Board. All ISPIRG publications, court actions, testimony, or other official representations of ISPIRG in the state must be approved by the State Board.

A staff member, through the State Board, may call on local boards for researchers on a particular issue. For example, if the Board were to decide that the enforcement of the Fair Credit Reporting Act needed evaluation, the staff could develop a research design for fact gathering and violation compilation to be done in the communities by students in the local boards. Such activities could be generated by the Student Board or a staff member could apply to the Board, explain the need and orientation of the project, and be assigned to the project.

Secondly, a local campus board may apply to the Board for technical and professional assistance. A staff member could be assigned to work with local researchers. The staff member can evaluate the research gathered to date and direct the researchers to additional sources of important information. They can work with students in formulating feasible solutions to identified problems and work toward implementation of those solutions.

What Role Will Individual Students Have in ISPIRG?

Individual students concerned about and committed to hard work to identify and solve specific citizen problems are the backbone of ISPIRG. Students working through their local board to analyze and formulate issues, gather facts, compile research findings, and develop alternative actions for problem solutions are integral to the success of ISPIRG.

Students acting out their role as concerned responsible citizens of a community, affected by public and private decisions, can and must have a voice in those decisions. The decisions made by corporate and governmental bodies have their impact at the local level; citizen advocacy must begin at that level.

What Kinds of Issues Will the Students Be Involved In?

ISPIRG can deal with any issues which the students deem crucial and which require investigation and action. The basic orientation of ISPIRG is consumer protection, environmental preservation, corporate and governmental responsibility. The organization views the concept of the environment in a broad, social context.

Within such a vast spectrum of public concern, students could research such things as the welfare system; property taxes; housing; automobile insurance; health care; legal services on campus; actions of state regulatory agencies; and many more.

Issues, research efforts, or project actions of the local board can be generated by member students and implemented by the board. The board can also provide research capabilities on common problems.

What Will the Staff Do?

Conduct research on projects approved by the State Board of Directors
Evaluate and supplement research done by the local boards
Translate analysis into action
a. testify before legislative hearings
b. participate in administrative rulemaking proceedings
c. disseminate information through press releases, public service spot announcements, and radio and t.v. appearances
d. publish books, pamphlets, and newsletters
e. prepare documentary films.
Consult with public and private decision-makers upon request
Engage in litigation
Assist in the development of college and university curriculum

How Will Issue Priorities Be Established?

On the local level the ability of a local board to assume new issues will be basically a function of student interest. If enough students have the time and ability to research a problem, such analysis can be undertaken.

Projects having state-wide implications or requiring staff assistance will be presented to and approved by the State Board of Directors prior to the assignment of professional staff or expenditure of funds. Any student can suggest to his or her local board issues that he or she feels require the attention of student researchers.

THE UNIVERSITY AND ISPIRG

How Does ISPIRG Relate to the Operation of the University?

First, a new "real problem" orientation may be injected into existing classes. There are presently few opportunities for students to work on existing social problems as part of their regular classwork. ISPIRG can work with both student and faculty in developing new focuses for classroom work.

Second, ISPIRG can also assist in developing new curriculum, stressing both a clinical approach to education and student participation in the community.

Third, by coordinating student efforts to the solution of public problems, ISPIRG will provide an additional means by which the University can meet its public service responsibilities. Iowa State University is a state-supported institution; the people of the state should receive some direct benefit from its operation.

What Is the Educational Value of ISPIRG to Students?

By participating in ISPIRG, students will become more aware of the problems in our society, the research required to understand those problems, the possibilities for their solution, and the means of solution-implementation. Students tend to have a heightened awareness of social ills while attending the University, but are rarely shown how such an awareness can be acted upon.

There is a definite gap between moral outrage and effective analysis and problem-solving. ISPIRG can assist students in placing issues of public concern in a workable context. Because research done for ISPIRG will be an integral part of a student's education, efforts will be made by the local boards to obtain academic credit for such research participation.

At Iowa State University it doesn't seem that this will be a very big problem. All faculty contacted thus far support this concept. If members of the faculty are willing to work with students, it is quite possible that credit can be given through the Special Problems category.

NC-PIRG

THE MEN WHO BROUGHT YOU

* CONSUMER FRAUD

* ENVIRONMENTAL DESTRUCTION

* CORPORATE IRRESPONSIBILITY

* GOVERNMENTAL UNRESPONSIVENESS

WILL NOT BRING YOU NC PIRG
ONLY STUDENTS CAN BRING NC PIRG

SIGN THE NC PIRG PETITION !

General Information

Students and professionals working together for necessary change

Funded, directed and controlled by students

A professional staff of scientists and attorneys

An active, full time force representing student concerns and public interest

Public Interest

ISPIRG will work for necessary change in areas that concern all of us:

- — environmental quality
- — consumer protection
- — racial and sexual discrimination
- — occupational safety
- — housing problems

An ombudsman for the public interest, reviewing activities of industry and government agencies

Student Support and Involvement

To fund ISPIRG operations, students throughout Iowa will petition to raise fees by $1.00 per quarter or $3.00 per year. Students who do not wish to participate will be entitled to a full cash refund at the beginning of each term.

ISPIRG will be controlled by an elected student board of directors. Students will work with the professionals at all levels of ISPIRG activity, including research, raising public awareness and support, drafting proposals, interacting with community groups and lobbying for legal changes.

Professional Staff

ISPIRG will hire a full time staff of 10-15 professionals, including:

- — lawyers
- — natural and social scientists
- — engineers and other experts in applied sciences

For more information, write ISPIRG, P.O. Box 1059, Des Moines, Iowa, 50311, or call your campus ISPIRG office.

ISPIRG

IOWA STUDENT PUBLIC INTEREST RESEARCH GROUP

How Would You Envision ISPIRG Operating a Year from Now?

Student investigators working with professionals can engage in rigorous analysis of public problems. They can carefully check the performance of various governmental agencies. They can monitor any hazardous products. They can act as public watchdogs for discrimination on the grounds of race, sex, or creed.

Local boards could and should undertake projects of a more or less local orientation. Expenditures and professional assistance for such projects must receive approval from the State Board.

When the existence of a particular problem has been fully documented and analyzed, ISPIRG will disseminate this information to the general public through press conferences and press releases, feature articles, radio and TV appearances, and public service spot announcements. ISPIRG can publish books, pamphlets, and newsletters. ISPIRG may prepare documentary filmstrips.

ISPIRG can testify before legislative hearings and participate in rule-making procedures of administrative agencies. Before making policy determinations, public officials responsible for those policy decisions and their subsequent enforcement should have available for consideration the most accurate and comprehensive data possible.

ISPIRG can constantly be available for consultation with public and private decision-makers. Armed with the facts turned up in the research efforts, public interest advocates can often dissuade decision makers from a course of action contrary to the public welfare.

Litigation is an effective, though expensive and time-consuming, course of action. It would almost certainly have to be directed by a staff member. Quite often courts are the only arenas in which to face squarely an unresponsible corporation or agency and, with good facts and thorough preparation, tremendous results can be reached through the courts.

Possibilities for extensive cooperation with participating schools in special educational and information programs will be explored. Universities and colleges have vast capabilities for reaching the general public through facilities such as educational programs, special conferences, seminars or guest lecturers. The use of university-operated radio and TV stations should be explored. The goal of such information dissemination is to create heightened public awareness of public problems.

Appendix 6
Sample Newspaper Coverage

OSPIRG SAYS: WATCH OUT FOR ASSOCIATED TIRE

An OSPIRG investigation of Portland car repair practices shows that a considerable number of shops here will sell the customer repairs he simply doesn't need.

Between December 1–9, two OSPIRG investigators from Portland State University made a total of 22 visits to 11 of the larger repair firms in the city. The cars they drove, a 1968 Chevelle and a 1969 Pontiac, had been thoroughly checked by instructors of the Automotive Education Schools of both Portland Community College and Mount Hood Community College. Both were certified in good running condition.

At each stop Elson Strahan and Ted Huff asked the mechanics to "check the front end." As their report—entitled "Automotive Suspension Diagnostic Practices in the Portland Metropolitan Area"—states, "59 per cent told us that work which was not needed should be done." Their report suggests that Portland car owners should especially beware of Associated Tire Centers, a national chain with 14 outlets in the Portland area. In eight visits to four different Associated Tire Centers, *the OSPIRG investigators were told each time that they needed expensive, unnecessary repairs and parts.*

On seven of eight visits to Associated Tire, they were told that their cars needed new tie-rod bushings. On five of the eight they were told to get new shock absorbers. Both had been okayed beforehand by independent mechanics.

The usual cost of bushings, as quoted by representatives of Associated Tire, was $33. New front end shock absorbers cost $27.50. Total cost of unnecessary bushings and shock absorbers recommended by the Associated Tire Centers was $394.75. (See the accompanying table for a detailed list of all visits made to Associated Tire.)

179

	1968 CHEVELLE License KFB 249	1969 PONTIAC License ADA 466
Assoc. Tire 5811 N.E. Sandy	New bushings ($33)	New bushings ($32.90)
Assoc. Tire 2002 S.E. Stark	New bushings ($16.95)	New bushings ($33) and shocks ($27.50)
Assoc. Tire 633 N.E. Broadway	New bushings ($32.95) and shocks ($27.50)	New bushings ($33) and shocks ($27.50)
Assoc. Tire 6841 N.E. Union	New front and rear shocks ($55)	New bushings ($33.95) and front and rear shocks ($69)

Both cars were checked and certified in good running order by automotive education instructors at local colleges. Tie-rods of both cars were found to be in excellent condition. All four shock absorbers on the Pontiac, and the two front shocks on the Chevelle were found to be in excellent condition. The rear shocks of the Chevelle were considered old and worn, but serviceable.

Strahan and Huff got the idea for their investigation from watching a CBS program on fraud in the auto repair business. As the show demonstrated, one ploy is to persuade the customer he needs new tie-rod bushings and shocks that are, in fact, in good shape. When a car is on the rack, a dishonest mechanic can turn the front wheels slightly and shake the tire in his hands. This is natural "give"; but the mechanic may frighten an unknowledgeable customer by telling him that it indicates a genuine hazard.

The Associated Tire Centers visited by the OSPIRG investigators were located at 5811 N.E. Sandy, 2002 S.E. Stark, 633 N.E. Broadway, and 6841 N.E. Union.

Strahan and Huff took both cars into a total of 11 Portland repair shops, including the Associated Tire Centers, and asked for safety checks. At two of the shops, Globe Brake Center, 936 S.E. Powell, and the Line-Up Shop, Inc., 834 S.E. Sandy, the cars were correctly diagnosed to be in excellent condition. Neither shop recommended any repairs. Of course, neither shop was aware of the OSPIRG investigation.

The OSPIRG office says that the B.F. Goodrich Store at 4003 S.E. 82nd should receive a special prize for spectacular inconsistency. An employee there, who found only probable re-alignment needed for the Chevelle, recommended a $177.25 repair job on the Pontiac, including an idler arm for $21.50, new shocks for $59.60, relining of the brakes for $49.95, a new cylinder for $34.00, and a new brake drum for $12.00.

Appendix 7
Sample of Enabling Legislation

ASSEMBLY CONCURRENT
RESOLUTION NO. 54

STATE OF NEW JERSEY

INTRODUCED FEBRUARY 14, 1972

By Assemblymen KEAN and KALTENBACHER

(Without Reference)

A CONCURRENT RESOLUTION endorsing the establishment of the New Jersey Public Interest Research Group (hereinafter referred to as NJPIRG) as a nonpartisan, nonprofit, student directed and financed corporation which will represent the concerns of New Jersey college and university students and work for constructive social change benefiting all New Jersey citizens in such areas as urban revitalization, consumer protection, occupational health and safety, environmental protection, racial and sexual discrimination, and similar areas of urgent and long-range concern.

1 WHEREAS, The energy and idealism of the university and college
2   students of the State of New Jersey are among the State's great
3   human resources; and

4 WHEREAS, Heretofore these same human resources have been
5   squandered and under-utilized through sporadic demonstrations
6   of concern and dissent; and

7 WHEREAS, The lack of institutional means for utilizing these same
8   resources has contributed to the rise of escapism and apathy
9   among college students and a loss to the State of these same
10   resources potentially adapted to the work of improving the con-
11   ditions of life for all of the citizens of New Jersey; and

183

12 WHEREAS, The methods and goals of NJPIRG will provide an in-
13   stitutional means for working within the established legal system;
14   and

15 WHEREAS, The educational goals of NJPIRG are in furtherance of
16   the public mandate to Rutgcrs, The State University, that it en-
17   gage in the higher education of the people of New Jersey; now,
18   therefore

1   BE IT RESOLVED *by the General Assembly (the Senate concurring):*
1   1. It is in the public interest of the people of the State of New
2   Jersey that NJPIRG be established to serve the purposes herein
3   described and as further defined in the NJPIRG corporate charter.